JAVASCRIPT
FOR
DUMMIES®

Quick Reference

by Emily Vander Veer

IDG Books Worldwide, Inc.
An International Data Group Company

Foster City, CA ✦ Chicago, IL ✦ Indianapolis, IN ✦ Southlake, TX

JavaScript™ For Dummies® Quick Reference

Published by
IDG Books Worldwide, Inc.
An International Data Group Company
919 E. Hillsdale Blvd.
Suite 400
Foster City, CA 94404
http://www.idgbooks.com (IDG Books Worldwide Web site)
http://www.dummies.com (Dummies Press Web site)

Library of Congress Catalog Card No.: 97-70368

ISBN: 0-7645-0112-7

Printed in the United States of America

10 9 8 7 6 5 4 3 2 1

1P/RU/QT/ZX/IN

Distributed in the United States by IDG Books Worldwide, Inc.

Distributed by Macmillan Canada for Canada; by Transworld Publishers Limited in the United Kingdom and Europe; by WoodsLane Pty. Ltd. for Australia; by WoodsLane Enterprises Ltd. for New Zealand; by Longman Singapore Publishers Ltd. for Singapore, Malaysia, Thailand, and Indonesia; by Simron Pty. Ltd. for South Africa; by Toppan Company Ltd. for Japan; by Distribuidora Cuspide for Argentina; by Livraria Cultura for Brazil; by Ediciencia S.A. for Ecuador; by Addison-Wesley Publishing Company for Korea; by Ediciones ZETA S.C.R. Ltda. for Peru; by WS Computer Publishing Company, Inc., for the Philippines; by Unalis Corporation for Taiwan; by Contemporanea de Ediciones for Venezuela. Authorized Sales Agent: Anthony Rudkin Associates for the Middle East and North Africa.

For general information on IDG Books Worldwide's books in the U.S., please call our Consumer Customer Service department at 800-762-2974. For reseller information, including discounts and premium sales, please call our Reseller Customer Service department at 800-434-3422.

For information on where to purchase IDG Books Worldwide's books outside the U.S., please contact our International Sales department at 415-655-3023 or fax 415-655-3299.

For information on foreign language translations, please contact our Foreign & Subsidiary Rights department at 415-655-3021 or fax 415-655-3281.

For sales inquiries and special prices for bulk quantities, please contact our Sales department at 415-655-3200 or write to the address above.

For information on using IDG Books Worldwide's books in the classroom or for ordering examination copies, please contact our Educational Sales department at 800-434-2086 or fax 817-251-8174.

For press review copies, author interviews, or other publicity information, please contact our Public Relations department at 415-655-3000 or fax 415-655-3299.

For authorization to photocopy items for corporate, personal, or educational use, please contact Copyright Clearance Center, 222 Rosewood Drive, Danvers, MA 01923, or fax 508-750-4470.

is a trademark under exclusive
license to IDG Books Worldwide, Inc.,
from International Data Group, Inc.

About the Author

Emily A. Vander Veer is the author of numerous magazine articles and computer books, including IDG Books Worldwide Inc.'s *JavaScript For Dummies* and *Java Beans For Dummies*. She is currently employed by IBM in Austin, Texas, where she focuses on writing about the very latest in Internet technology.

When she's not scribbling on her virtual tablet, Emily enjoys concocting lavish ethnic meals (to the delight of her adopted stray cat and Australian shepherd mix pooches, who fortunately will eat just about anything!).

Contact Emily at emilyv@vnet.ibm.com.

ABOUT IDG BOOKS WORLDWIDE

Welcome to the world of IDG Books Worldwide.

IDG Books Worldwide, Inc., is a subsidiary of International Data Group, the world's largest publisher of computer-related information and the leading global provider of information services on information technology. IDG was founded more than 25 years ago and now employs more than 8,500 people worldwide. IDG publishes more than 275 computer publications in over 75 countries (see listing below). More than 60 million people read one or more IDG publications each month.

Launched in 1990, IDG Books Worldwide is today the #1 publisher of best-selling computer books in the United States. We are proud to have received eight awards from the Computer Press Association in recognition of editorial excellence and three from *Computer Currents'* First Annual Readers' Choice Awards. Our best-selling *...For Dummies®* series has more than 30 million copies in print with translations in 30 languages. IDG Books Worldwide, through a joint venture with IDG's Hi-Tech Beijing, became the first U.S. publisher to publish a computer book in the People's Republic of China. In record time, IDG Books Worldwide has become the first choice for millions of readers around the world who want to learn how to better manage their businesses.

Our mission is simple: Every one of our books is designed to bring extra value and skill-building instructions to the reader. Our books are written by experts who understand and care about our readers. The knowledge base of our editorial staff comes from years of experience in publishing, education, and journalism — experience we use to produce books for the '90s. In short, we care about books, so we attract the best people. We devote special attention to details such as audience, interior design, use of icons, and illustrations. And because we use an efficient process of authoring, editing, and desktop publishing our books electronically, we can spend more time ensuring superior content and spend less time on the technicalities of making books.

You can count on our commitment to deliver high-quality books at competitive prices on topics you want to read about. At IDG Books Worldwide, we continue in the IDG tradition of delivering quality for more than 25 years. You'll find no better book on a subject than one from IDG Books Worldwide.

John Kilcullen
CEO
IDG Books Worldwide, Inc.

Eighth Annual
Computer Press
Awards ≥1992

Ninth Annual
Computer Press
Awards ≥1993

Tenth Annual
Computer Press
Awards ≥1994

Eleventh Annual
Computer Press
Awards ≥1995

IDG Books Worldwide, Inc., is a subsidiary of International Data Group, the world's largest publisher of computer-related information and the leading global provider of information services on information technology. International Data Group publishes over 275 computer publications in over 75 countries. Sixty million people read one or more International Data Group publications each month. International Data Group's publications include: ARGENTINA: Buyer's Guide, Computerworld Argentina, PC World Argentina; AUSTRALIA: Australian Macworld, Australian PC World, Australian Reseller News, Computerworld, IT Casebook, Network World, Publish, Webmaster; AUSTRIA: Computerwelt Osterreich, Networks Austria, PC Tip Austria; BANGLADESH: PC World Bangladesh; BELARUS: PC World Belarus; BELGIUM: Data News; BRAZIL: Annuário de Informática, Computerworld, Connections, Macworld, PC Player, PC World, Publish, Reseller News, Supergamepower; BULGARIA: Computerworld Bulgaria, Network World Bulgaria, PC & MacWorld Bulgaria; CANADA: CIO Canada, Client/Server World, ComputerWorld Canada, InfoWorld Canada, NetworkWorld Canada, WebWorld; CHILE: Computerworld Chile, PC World Chile; COLOMBIA: Computerworld Colombia, PC World Colombia; COSTA RICA: PC World Centro America; THE CZECH AND SLOVAK REPUBLICS: Computerworld Czechoslovakia, Macworld Czech Republic, PC World Czechoslovakia; DENMARK: Communications World Danmark, Computerworld Danmark, Macworld Danmark, PC World Danmark, Techworld Denmark; DOMINICAN REPUBLIC: PC World Republica Dominicana; ECUADOR: PC World Ecuador; EGYPT: Computerworld Middle East, PC World Middle East; EL SALVADOR: PC World Centro America; FINLAND: MikroPC, Tietoverkko, Tietoviikko; FRANCE: Distributique, Hebdo, Info PC, Le Monde Informatique, Macworld, Reseaux & Telecoms, WebMaster France; GERMANY: Computer Partner, Computerwoche, Computerwoche Extra, Computerwoche FOCUS, Global Online, Macwelt, PC Welt; GREECE: Amiga Computing, GamePro Greece, Multimedia World; GUATEMALA: PC World Centro America; HONDURAS: PC World Centro America; HONG KONG: Computerworld Hong Kong, PC World Hong Kong, Publish in Asia; HUNGARY: ABCD CD-ROM, Computerworld Szamitastechnika, Internetto online Magazine, PC World Hungary, PC-X Magazin Hungary; ICELAND: Tolvuheimur PC World Island; INDIA: Information Communications World, Information Systems Computerworld, PC World India, Publish in Asia; INDONESIA: InfoKomputer PC World, Komputek Computerworld, Publish in Asia; IRELAND: ComputerScope, PC Live!; ISRAEL: Macworld Israel, People & Computers/Computerworld; ITALY: Computerworld Italia, Macworld Italia, Networking Italia, PC World Italia; JAPAN: DTP World, Macworld Japan, Nikkei Personal Computing, OS/2 World Japan, SunWorld Japan, Windows NT World, Windows World Japan; KENYA: PC World East African; KOREA: Hi-Tech Information, Macworld Korea, PC World Korea; MACEDONIA: PC World Macedonia; MALAYSIA: Computerworld Malaysia, PC World Malaysia, Publish in Asia; MALTA: PC World Malta; MEXICO: Computerworld Mexico, PC World Mexico; MYANMAR: PC World Myanmar; NETHERLANDS: Computer! Totaal, LAN Internetworking Magazine, LAN World Buyers Guide, Macworld Netherlands, Net, WebWereld; NEW ZEALAND: Absolute Beginners Guide and Plain & Simple Series, Computer Buyer, Computer Industry Directory, Computerworld New Zealand, MTB, Network World, PC World New Zealand; NICARAGUA: PC World Centro America; NORWAY: Computerworld Norge, CW Rapport, Datamagasinet, Financial Rapport, Kursguide Norge, Macworld Norge, Multimediaworld Norge, PC World Ekspress Norge, PC World Nettverk, PC World Norge, PC World ProduktGuide Norge; PAKISTAN: Computerworld Pakistan; PANAMA: PC World Panama; PEOPLE'S REPUBLIC OF CHINA: China Computer Users, China Computerworld, China InfoWorld, China Telecom World Weekly, Computer & Communication, Electronic Design China, Electronics Today, Electronics Weekly, Game Software, PC World China, Popular Computer Week, Software Weekly, Software World, Telecom World; PERU: Computerworld Peru, PC World Profesional Peru, PC World SoHo Peru; PHILIPPINES: Click!, Computerworld Philippines, PC World Philippines, Publish in Asia; POLAND: Computerworld Poland, Computerworld Special Report Poland, Cyber, Macworld Poland, Networld Poland, PC World Komputer; PORTUGAL: Cerebro/PC World, Computerworld/Correio Informático, Dealer World Portugal, Mac*In/PC*In Portugal, Multimedia World; PUERTO RICO: PC World Puerto Rico; ROMANIA: Computerworld Romania, PC World Romania, Telecom Romania; RUSSIA: Computerworld Russia, Mir PK, Publish, Seti; SINGAPORE: Computerworld Singapore, PC World Singapore, Publish in Asia; SLOVENIA: Monitor; SOUTH AFRICA: Computing SA, Network World SA, Software World SA; SPAIN: Communicaciones World España, Computerworld España, Macworld España, PC World España, PC World Gaming; SRI LANKA: Infolink PC World; SWEDEN: CAP&Design, Computer Sweden, Corporate Computing Sweden, Internetworld Sweden, it.branschen, Macworld Sweden, MaxiData Sweden, MikroDatorn, Natverk & Kommunikation, PC World Sweden, PCaktiv, Windows World Sweden; SWITZERLAND: Computerworld Schweiz, Macworld Schweiz, PCtip; TAIWAN: Computerworld Taiwan, Macworld Taiwan, NEW ViSiON/Publish, PC World Taiwan, Windows World Taiwan; THAILAND: Publish in Asia, Thai Computerworld; TURKEY: Computerworld Turkiye, Macworld Turkiye, PC World Turkiye; UKRAINE: Computerworld Kiev, Multimedia World Ukraine, PC World Ukraine; UNITED KINGDOM: Acorn User UK, Amiga Action UK, Amiga Computing UK, Apple Talk UK, Computing, Macworld, Parents and Computers UK, PC Advisor, PC Home, PSX Pro, The WEB; UNITED STATES: Cable in the Classroom, CIO Magazine, Computerworld, DOS World, Federal Computer Week, GamePro Magazine, InfoWorld, I-Way, Macworld, Network World, PC Games, PC World, Publish, Video Event, THE WEB Magazine, and WebMaster; online webzines: JavaWorld, NetscapeWorld, and SunWorld Online; URUGUAY: InfoWorld Uruguay; VENEZUELA: Computerworld Venezuela, PC World Venezuela; and VIETNAM: PC World Vietnam.   1/24/97

Dedication

To my husband, Clay, whose tireless forays into the Austin wilderness for "just one more pint of Ben & Jerry's" during the writing of this book were greatly appreciated.

Author's Acknowledgments

Many thanks to Gareth Hancock, for giving me the opportunity to write this book, and to the other IDG Books' staff members who worked on this project: Kathy Cox, my project editor, and Joe Jansen, my copy editor. Both of these folks provided me with invaluable suggestions and advice and made writing this book much more fun than it would have been otherwise. Thanks also to the Production and Proofreading staff for the well-crafted final product.

I'd also like to thank my colleagues at IBM, for whose generosity and support during the writing of this book I am humbly grateful.

Publisher's Acknowledgments

We're proud of this book; please send us your comments about it by using the Reader Response Card at the back of the book or by e-mailing us at feedback/dummies@idgbooks.com. Some of the people who helped bring this book to market include the following:

Acquisitions, Development, and Editorial

Project Editor: Kathleen M. Cox

Acquisitions Editor: Gareth Hancock

Product Development Manager: Mary Bednarek

Copy Editor: Joe Jansen

Technical Editor: Greg Guntle

Editorial Manager: Mary C. Corder

Editorial Assistant: Michael D. Sullivan

Production

Project Coordinator: Sherry Gomoll

Layout and Graphics: Brett Black, Cameron Booker, J. Tyler Connor, Angela F. Hunckler, Drew R. Moore, Brent Savage

Proofreaders: Kathy McGuinnes, Joel Draper, Nancy Price, Rob Springer

Indexer: Lori Lathrop

Special Help: E. Shawn Aylsworth

General and Administrative

IDG Books Worldwide, Inc.: John Kilcullen, CEO; Steven Berkowitz, President and Publisher

IDG Books Technology Publishing: Brenda McLaughlin, Senior Vice President and Group Publisher

Dummies Technology Press and Dummies Editorial: Diane Graves Steele, Vice President and Associate Publisher; Judith A. Taylor, Brand Manager; Kristin A. Cocks, Editorial Director

Dummies Trade Press: Kathleen A. Welton, Vice President and Publisher; Stacy S. Collins, Brand Manager

IDG Books Production for Dummies Press: Beth Jenkins, Production Director; Cindy L. Phipps, Supervisor of Project Coordination, Production Proofreading, and Indexing; Kathie S. Schutte, Supervisor of Page Layout; Shelley Lea, Supervisor of Graphics and Design; Debbie J. Gates, Production Systems Specialist; Tony Augsburger, Supervisor of Reprints and Bluelines; Leslie Popplewell, Media Archive Coordinator

Dummies Packaging and Book Design: Patti Sandez, Packaging Specialist; Lance Kayser, Packaging Assistant; Kavish+Kavish, Cover Design

♦

The publisher would like to give special thanks to Patrick J. McGovern, without whom this book would not have been possible.

♦

Table of Contents

Part VII: Properties (Object Data) 125

How to Use This Book

You loved the book (*JavaScript For Dummies,* that is), and you saw the movie six times. You want to use JavaScript to add flash and interactivity to your Web pages and, more than likely, you have a pretty good idea of how you want to go about it. Still, you could use a handy reference manual to keep nearby for those times when you know *what* you want to do, but can't remember exactly *how* to do it. Well, you're in luck! Because you're obviously reading this, congratulate yourself: You've found the most complete, down-to-earth JavaScript reference available in this or any other galaxy.

Unlike some reference works that are technically correct but hopelessly detailed, this book offers tons of working examples of how to do the things you *really* want to do with JavaScript, like adding multimedia and interactive input forms to your Web pages.

JavaScript For Dummies Quick Reference gives you a bare-bones HTML primer that explains the subset of HTML statements that are absolutely indispensable to a JavaScripter, followed by a comprehensive review of the JavaScript language itself and an in-depth look at the JavaScript object model — every last object, property, method, event handler, and function available in JavaScript.

Relating JavaScript to the World Wide Web

The World Wide Web (from now on out, called just plain *Web*) is an extremely complex animal. There's so much to know — from communication protocols to browsers, from HTML to JavaScript to Java, and other proprietary architectures and platforms. Unfortunately, most of these technologies are described and documented as though they exist in a vacuum, which leaves the average intelligent person curious about the *big* picture: How does it all fit together? If that's a tree, what does the forest look like? In short, what's it all about, Alfie?

You really don't have to be a rocket scientist to understand this JavaScript stuff — all you need is an overview in plain English. Here, then, is a birds-eye view of the role JavaScript plays in this brave new world of Web application development.

The Internet

In the beginning, there was the Internet: A huge (and I mean *huge*) conglomeration of networked computers. At first, you *did* have to be a rocket scientist (or at least a computer scientist) to access the Internet, because its interface was so cryptic and unfriendly to humans. That all changed with the advent of the Internet *protocols* that formed the World Wide Web.

The World Wide Web

The Web runs primarily on two protocols:

+ HTML *(HyperText Markup Language):* The language in which Web pages are written

+ HTTP *(HyperText Transfer Protocol):* The special way of communicating that lets computers like *Web servers* and *Web clients* shuttle Web pages back and forth

A *Web server* is an industrial-strength computer, usually running UNIX or Windows NT. Web servers hold peoples' Web pages and hang around waiting for requests. A *Web client* is a regular computer (usually a PC or a Macintosh) that has Web *browser* software installed on it — browsers like Netscape Navigator or Microsoft Internet Explorer that hunt and peck through cyberspace at your command.

When you use your favorite Web browser to load a Web page, such as the one denoted by the URL *(Uniform Resource Locator)* `http://www.dummies.com`, your browser fetches the page from wherever it is on the Web and brings it to your browser. Your browser then interprets the fetched HTML file and displays it for you in living color.

JavaScript the Magnificent

Where does JavaScript come in? JavaScript is a scripting language designed by Sun Microsystems, Inc. A *scripting language* is a limited programming language designed to extend the capabilities of another application. The JavaScript language is an extension to HTML and lets you create interactive Web pages. With JavaScript-enabled Web pages, users can press buttons, type text, perform calculations, and call Java programs or plug-ins — without a whole lot of programming effort. (Other ways exist to create interactive Web pages, notably by using *server-side scripting* by means of *CGI*, or *Common Gateway Interface* programs. But I'm here to tell you, you're back to needing a PhD in astrophysics when you start dabbling around with CGI.)

At the time of this writing, JavaScript is supported by Netscape Navigator 3.0 and Internet Explorer 3.0. (I say that these browsers *support* JavaScript because they have JavaScript interpreters built into them.) Yet, while Netscape Navigator and Internet Explorer both support JavaScript, their implementations differ slightly. I alert you throughout the book when I cover topics that the two browsers handle differently. To be on the safe side, you should always test your JavaScript-enabled Web pages on both Web browsers before you send them out into the big wide world.

The JavaScript implementations on various Web browsers have been known to change slightly from version to version (for example, from Netscape Navigator 2.0 to 3.0) — so you can probably expect this situation to continue in the future. What this fact means to you as a JavaScript author is that it's a good idea to test your JavaScript-enabled Web pages on the new Web browser versions as soon as they become available. You want to make sure that the Web pages that you created for the older Web browser still work on the newer version. After all, if users attempt to load your Web page and it tanks, you're the one they'll blame!

Finding Exactly What You're Looking for in This Book

This book is organized so that you can find information quickly, either by browsing through the main sections (described in the following paragraphs) or by looking through the alphabetized Table of Contents.

Part I, "First Things First: Creating HTML Objects to Work within JavaScript," presents the basic HTML statements that you need to create a basic Web page from scratch. Many of the statements create the actual HTML elements, or *objects,* which you can change, look at, display, and otherwise manipulate with JavaScript statements.

Part II, "JavaScript Basics," presents the JavaScript object model and shows you how to reference each object in the object hierarchy. This part also introduces the JavaScript keywords, explains how you can use each keyword, and describes the syntax you need to follow to create valid JavaScript statements.

Part III, "HTML Objects: The Heart of It All," gives you a blow-by-blow analysis of all of the HTML objects available to you in JavaScript (in other words, the ones you learn how to create in Part II). This part, together with parts IV, V, VI, VII, and VIII, provide you a complete JavaScript language reference.

Part IV, "Data Types: Building Basic JavaScript Objects," shows you how to put the most basic JavaScript objects into your Web pages. This part covers the JavaScript objects that you're likely to include in almost every script you're likely to write — objects like Array, Date, Function, Option, and String. This part shows you the correct syntax for including basic objects in your scripts and even gives you examples of working JavaScript code.

Part V, "Functions" lists all of JavaScript's built-in functions, describes how to use functions to create instances of objects, and clues you in on how to custom-design your own functions.

Part VI, "Methods: How an Object Behaves," shows you all you'd ever want to know about methods. This part gives you a rundown of every method available to you in the JavaScript library, demonstrates the proper way to call each method, and gives you easy-to-understand code examples and explanations.

Part VII, "Properties (Object Data)" is an exhaustive listing of the items that represent an object's data — its properties. This part tells you how to access and modify object properties and relates those properties to their corresponding HTML tag attributes.

Part VIII, "Event Handlers," shows you how to use these special attributes to specify JavaScript statements (typically you'll specify just one statement — a function call) for the browser to invoke automatically whenever an event occurs.

Part IX, "Cool Things You Can Do with JavaScript," shows you how to do all the stuff you really want to do with JavaScript — things like adding multimedia action to your Web pages, creating interactive controls, validating user input, and calling other (non-JavaScript) components from your JavaScript scripts. In this part, you find instructions for everything from loading a JavaScript-enabled Web page (which is dead-easy) to interacting with cookies (a considerably more advanced topic).

Appendix A, "Reserved Words," briefs you on the JavaScript keywords that you need to avoid when you name your variables and functions.

Appendix B, "Color Values," contains a list of predefined shades that you can use to color the background (or any other part) of your Web page.

The glossary, called "Techie Talk," appears at the very end of the book. You can check this part to look up words you're not familiar with, or that you've come across before but have forgotten.

Understanding the Conventions Used in This Book

HTML and JavaScript code appear in this book in monospaced font, like this line of HTML code:

```
<TITLE>My First JavaScript-Enabled Web Page</TITLE>
```

Make sure that you follow word-for-word the syntax in the examples (that is, the spacing, capitalization, and spelling). Some variations may work, but some won't — and consistency pays big dividends in reading your code later. The exception to this syntax rule relates to italicized words, which act as placeholders for other values, which you can substitute in your actual code. For example, in the following line of JavaScript code, you can replace myCatName and "Scooter Pie" with other values, but you need to type var exactly the way it appears:

var *myCatName* = "*Scooter Pie*"

If you need to type something in, the directive appears in boldface, like this:

Type **return**.

I also use boldface to highlight lines of code I refer to in the text.

Due to the narrow margins of this book, sometimes code examples may wrap around from one line to another. JavaScript doesn't require a line continuation character, so you can copy the code exactly as it appears, *unless* the break occurs between two quotes, like this:

```
var favoriteActivity = "sleeping late on
Sundays"  // Warning! Invalid break
```

And finally, because JavaScript scripts don't exist in a vacuum (you must integrate your JavaScript scripts into HTML files), you see two different types of coding statements in this book:

✦ HTML statements

✦ JavaScript statements

The conventions listed in the preceding paragraphs are all you need to follow to create customized, working JavaScript statements on your own computer. HTML statements, however, tend to be a little more daunting until you're familiar with them. The following code shows the correct syntax for an HTML statement, and the following table explains the HTML elements in more detail. Here's how you make sense of HTML syntax:

```
<TAG-NAME [ATTRIBUTE[="VALUE"]...]>[some text]
  [</TAG-NAME>]
```

HTML Syntax Element	Meaning
<	Angle brackets (<>) surround a tag name.
TAG-NAME	Tag names are HTML keywords like TITLE, SCRIPT, and INPUT.
[	Square brackets surround items that are optional (depending on the tag name that you're working with).
ATTRIBUTE	Attributes are associated with specific tag names. For example, the TYPE attribute is associated with the INPUT tag.
="VALUE"	Some attributes require values. For example, the TYPE attribute of the INPUT tag requires a value which could be BUTTON, RESET, SUBMIT, or some other predefined value.

HTML Syntax Element	Meaning
. . .	The ellipses (...) mean that some tags require multiple attribute-value pairs. For example, the INPUT tag definition may include `TYPE="BUTTON"` and `NAME="myButton"`
[some text]	Some tags require associated text; for example, the `OPTION` tag (which defines an entry in a `SELECT` list box) requires you to specify some descriptive text for the entry to display to the user.
</TAG-NAME>	Some tags require a closing tag, like this: `<TITLE>Some title</TITLE>`

Figuring Out What the Icons Mean

To make your life easier (as it relates to JavaScript, at least!), I include a few icons to give you a heads-up on practical scripting-related tidbits:

 This icon indicates a handy cross-reference to some other . . .*For Dummies* book that explains the related topic in lots more detail.

 This icon alerts you to handy tricks and techniques that can save you time, hassle, and many, many tufts of hair.

 Next to this icon are common pitfalls, bugs, and assorted "uh-ohs" to look out for.

 This icon points out items that don't work the way you'd expect them to — a touch of illogic in the normally logical world of computerdom.

 This icon marks a faster way that you might choose to accomplish a task — saving you valuable time and keystrokes.

 This icon flags Web sites that you can visit for more in-depth information on a related topic.

 Rejoice when you see this icon! It indicates real-live, working JavaScript/HTML source code.

Where to Go from Here

Because JavaScript gives you instant feedback, it's really fun to use (okay, it's fun compared to other programming languages — maybe not compared to a two-week beach vacation!). To get the most out of this book, you may want to try creating a Web page from scratch and then adding to it a piece at a time as ideas occur to you. Take the afternoon off, kick the dogs out, and experiment with some of the suggestions in this book. If you get stuck, just flip to the section that covers whatever's giving you a hard time, copy the example you'll find there, and modify it until it's just the way you want it. Creating incredible Web pages with JavaScript isn't illegal, immoral, or fattening, so what are you waiting for? Go for it!

> To get some troubleshooting tips if you get an error message on your JavaScript code, check out the *JavaScript For Dummies Quick Reference* page on the Dummies Web site at `http://www.Dummies.com`

First Things First: Creating HTML Objects to Work within JavaScript

JavaScript is an ultra-pared-down, ultra-easy programming language specifically designed to make Web page elements *interactive*. An *interactive* element is one that responds to user input — for example, a push button that causes something to happen when a user clicks on it, or a text field that automatically checks the accuracy of text that a user types in. In order to make elements interactive, though, the elements first have to exist. For elements to exist, you have to create them — which you can do easily with HTML statements like the ones in this part.

In this part . . .

✔ Creating a basic, no-nonsense Web page in HTML

✔ Adding elements to your Web page

✔ Connecting your Web page to a server-side CGI program

Creating a Meat-and-Potatoes Web Page

Creating a Web page is a fairly simple process, as you can see in this overview. (The rest of this part shows you exactly how to implement each phase of the overview.)

First, you need to create an HTML document file called `someFile.html` (or, if your system doesn't support long filename extensions, name your file `someFile.htm`). You can use whichever text editor you're most comfortable with to create the HTML file, such as WordPad, BBEdit, the text editor that's included as part of Netscape Navigator Gold, or even your favorite word processor package — as long as the program lets you save plain text. The HTML document that you create should have the following sections:

✦ **The overall document section (required):** In order for the HTML interpreter to recognize that your document is an HTML file and not just any old file, the document file's first line must contain the beginning `<HTML>` tag, and the last line must contain the ending `</HTML>` tag. All the other HTML tags and JavaScript statements you decide to incorporate into your Web page are optional — but whichever tags or statements you include must appear between the `<HTML>...</HTML>` tags.

✦ **The header section (optional):** If your document has a header (such as "Creating a Meat-and-Potatoes Web Page," which you see at the beginning of this section), the header immediately follows the beginning `<HTML>` tag. The header is bounded by the opening `<HEAD>` tag and the closing `</HEAD>` tag. You *must* place some elements inside the header, such as your Web page's title. Other elements — for example, a JavaScript script, which is identified by the `<SCRIPT>` tag — may or may not take up residence in the header.

✦ **The body section (technically optional but practically required!):** You *could* create a document that doesn't contain a body, but it would be pretty boring! All the interactive form elements that you become familiar with in this part must appear between the `<BODY>...</BODY>` tags in order to be recognized by the HTML interpreter.

See also "Getting Started with a Bare-Bones HTML Template," in Part IX, which contains a mini-HTML file with the document, header, body, and script tags already in place.

After you create an HTML document file, you can load the page in any JavaScript-enabled Web browser (for example, Netscape Navigator or Microsoft Internet Explorer) and view your new Web page.

When you finish testing your Web page and it looks absolutely perfect, you'll probably want to share it with the world — which requires giving your document file (and perhaps some cash) to a Web server administrator. *Creating Web Pages For Dummies,* by Bud Smith and Arthur Bebak (published by IDG Books Worldwide, Inc.), contains a whole chapter describing free (!) and easy ways to get your page up and running on the Web.

Body section: <BODY> . . . </BODY>

Typically, the body of the document is where most of the HTML statements live — smack-dab between the `<BODY>...</BODY>` tag pairs.

To define a body section in HTML, use this tag pair:
`<BODY>...</BODY>`

To access that body section in JavaScript, use this identifier:
`document`

The `<BODY>...</BODY>` tag pair, itself, gives you the opportunity to customize the colors that your Web page displays.

You can change the color of any of the items that appear in the Description column of the following table to any of the color values shown in Appendix B.

Setting Colors in HTML	Description	Accessing Colors in JavaScript
`BGCOLOR="chartreuse"`	Background page color	`document.bgColor`
`TEXT="blue"`	Foreground (text) color	`document.fgColor`
`LINK="yellow"`	Link color before it's clicked	`document.linkColor`
`ALINK="white"`	Link color as it's being clicked	`document.alinkColor`
`VLINK="black"`	Link color after it's been clicked	`document.vlinkColor`

Here's how the code in the preceding table might look when you set up the body of an HTML document:

```
<HTML>
. . .
<BODY
BGCOLOR="someColor"
TEXT="someColor"
LINK="someColor"
ALINK="someColor"
VINK="someColor">
. . .
```

```
Most of your HTML code, including code for your
    interactive form, goes right here.
...
</BODY>
</HTML>
```

Header section: <HEAD> . . . </HEAD>

Because the JavaScript interpreter (the software bundled with some Web browsers that enables the browser to recognize JavaScript statements) begins reading the HTML code at the top of each file and works downward, the <HEAD> tag should appear near the top of the file:

```
<HTML>
<HEAD>
Statements placed here are interpreted as soon
as the Web page is loaded.
</HEAD>
...
The bulk of your HTML statements, including your
    body section, goes here.
...
</HTML>
```

Take advantage of the organizational convenience of the header and body sections of an HTML document. For example, if you make a habit of putting all your JavaScript function definitions in the header section, you can be sure that your functions will be available to the rest of your Web page.

Interactive form: <FORM> . . . </FORM>

The <FORM>...</FORM> tag pair is arguably one of the most important tags you can use, JavaScript maven *fantastique*. The <FORM> tag surrounds the heart of the JavaScript-enabled Web page: the interactive form. A form is used to gather input from users and to send, or *post,* form data to a server for additional processing. You always define forms inside the <BODY>... </BODY> section.

To define a form in HTML, use this tag pair:
`<FORM NAME="myForm">...</FORM>`

To access that form in JavaScript, use this identifier:
`document.myForm`

You must place the tag for any form element you choose to include in your Web page, be it a button, a list box, a text field, or whatever, between the <FORM>...</FORM> tags, as shown in the following table:

Tag Syntax for `<FORM>`	*Explanation*
`<FORM`	Opening `<FORM>` tag
`NAME="formName"`	Internal name of form (for coding purposes)
`[TARGET="windowName"]`	Window to display server response (optional; default is current window)
`[ACTION="serverURL"]`	URL where form data is sent when the user submits the form (optional)
`[METHOD=GET | POST]`	Data send method is either `GET` or `POST`; `GET` is default (optional)
`[ENCTYPE="encodingType"]`	Special data encoding scheme, if any (optional)
`[onSubmit="handlerText"]>`	Code to invoke when form is submitted (optional)
`...`	Put all your form elements here
`</FORM>`	Closing `<FORM>` tag

See also "Inserting Form Elements into Your Web Page," later in this part, which defines form elements like buttons, text fields, and list boxes.

You may never take advantage of all the stuff in the syntax; at least, not until you become an expert! To get you started, here's a common, everyday example of the syntax for an interactive form:

```
<FORM NAME="myForm">
...
<INPUT TYPE="button" NAME="calculatePrice"
    VALUE="Calculate Now!"
    onClick="calculatePrice()">
...
</FORM>
```

The syntax for HTML in general, and the `<INPUT>` tag in particular, can be a little intimidating if you're not familiar with it. For the whole scoop on HTML syntax, check out *HTML For Dummies,* 2nd Edition, by Ed Tittel and Steve James.

JavaScript script: <SCRIPT> ... </SCRIPT>

The `<SCRIPT>...</SCRIPT>` HTML tag pair lets you insert a JavaScript script into your Web page. (Be aware that JavaScript isn't the only scripting language that you can specify; that's why the `<SCRIPT>` tag has an associated `LANGUAGE` attribute.) You can place a JavaScript script inside the header or the body section of your Web page, and you can insert as many scripts as you want. (**See also** Part IX for some cool script ideas.)

Because JavaScript is an object-based (*not* object-oriented) language, the JavaScript code you write will be rife with references to entities such as *objects, methods,* and *properties.* Unfortunately, due to space constraints, this book doesn't contain a discussion of object-based programming. If you're interested in object-based programming, concepts, and techniques (especially with respect to JavaScript), pick up a copy of *JavaScript For Dummies,* by Emily Vander Veer (that's me, by the way).

Tag Syntax for `<SCRIPT>`	*Explanation*
`<SCRIPT`	Opening `<SCRIPT>` tag
`[LANGUAGE="JavaScript"]`	Scripting language (optional but recommended; `JavaScript` is the default)
`[SRC="fileName.js"]>`	JavaScript source filename (optional)
`...`	Your JavaScript statements go here *unless* you specify a value for `SRC`
`</SCRIPT>`	Closing `</SCRIPT>` tag

Here's an example of the `<SCRIPT>` tag in action, just to get you started:

```
<HTML>
<SCRIPT LANGUAGE="JavaScript">
...
</SCRIPT>
</HTML>
```

Make sure that you don't place HTML statements inside the `<SCRIPT>...</SCRIPT>` tags. The only statements that the JavaScript interpreter considers valid between these two tags are JavaScript statements — any other type of statement causes a syntax error.

Web page: <HTML> . . . </HTML>

Some browsers may load your HTML document file just to find out if either or both of these tags are missing. Technically, though, the Web browsers don't have to — and there's no guarantee that they'll keep doing so in the future. So, to be on the safe side, always include the `<HTML>...</HTML>` tag pair in your HTML document file. The beginning tag should be the first line in your file, and the ending tag should be the last line, as shown in the following example:

```
<HTML>
Place any HTML or JavaScript statements that you
    choose to include in your HTML file between
    these tags.
</HTML>
```

Inserting Form Elements into Your Web Page

All the elements described in this section are form elements and, because they're part of a form, they must be defined between the `<FORM>`...`</FORM>` tags which, in turn, must be defined between the `<BODY>`...`</BODY>` tags. Read on for specific examples.

ActiveX component: <OBJECT> . . . </OBJECT>

ActiveX components are currently compatible only with Internet Explorer's version of JavaScript, but rumor has it that ActiveX compatibility is coming soon to Navigator.

To embed an ActiveX component in an HTML document, use this tag pair: `<OBJECT>`...`</OBJECT>`

To access that ActiveX component in the Internet Explorer implementation of JavaScript, use this identifier: `document.myForm.myActiveXId`

The ink on the `<OBJECT>` tag specification isn't even close to being dry at the time of this writing, which means that the information in this section may have changed slightly by the time you read this. To keep up with the official `<OBJECT>` tag goings-on, keep an eye on the following URL:

`http://www.w3.org/pub/WWW/TR/WD-object.html#object`

Tag Syntax for Embedded ActiveX Component	Explanation
`<OBJECT`	Opening `<OBJECT>` tag
`CLASSID="classid"`	Classid of the component
`ID="componentId"`	Internal name of component for coding purposes
`[HEIGHT="pixels" | "value"%]`	Height of the component, in pixels or as a percentage of the window height
`[WIDTH="pixels" | "value"%]`	Width of the component, in pixels or as a percentage of the window height
`[HSPACE="pixels"]`	Horizontal space between left and right sides of the component and left and right edges of the window, in pixels

(continued)

Tag Syntax for Embedded ActiveX Component	Explanation
[VSPACE="pixels"]	Vertical space between top and bottom of component and top and bottom edges of the window, in pixels
[ALIGN="position"]>	Specifies alignment of image
You can repeat the following optional section as many times as necessary:	
[<PARAM	Opening <PARAM> tag
NAME="parameterName"	Name of parameter to pass to component
VALUE="parameterValue">]	Value to pass to component
[</PARAM>]	Closing <PARAM> tag
</OBJECT>	Closing </OBJECT> tag

The following code embeds an ActiveX component whose purpose in life is to load a Web page (in this example, the IDG Books Worldwide home page). This code then flips the Web page around and around inside a skinny little horizontal window.

```
<OBJECT
  ALIGN=CENTER
  CLASSID="clsid:1a4da620-6217-11cf-be62-
    0080c72edd2d"
  WIDTH=650 HEIGHT=40 BORDER=1 HSPACE=5
  ID=marquee>
  <PARAM NAME="ScrollStyleX" VALUE="Circular">
  <PARAM NAME="ScrollStyleY" VALUE="Circular">
  <PARAM NAME="szURL" VALUE="http://
    www.idgbooks.com">
  <PARAM NAME="ScrollDelay" VALUE=100>
  <PARAM NAME="LoopsX" VALUE=->
  <PARAM NAME="LoopsY" VALUE=->
  <PARAM NAME="ScrollPixelsX" VALUE=0>
  <PARAM NAME="ScrollPixelsY" VALUE=30>
  <PARAM NAME="DrawImmediately" VALUE=1>
  <PARAM NAME="Whitespace" VALUE=0>
  <PARAM NAME="PageFlippingOn" VALUE=1>
  <PARAM NAME="Zoom" VALUE=100>
  <PARAM NAME="WidthOfPage" VALUE=640>
  </OBJECT>
```

Graphic image: <IMG>

To embed an image in HTML, use this tag:
```
<IMG NAME="myImage"...>
```

To access that image in Navigator's implementation of JavaScript, use this identifier: document.myForm.myImage.

You can embed any image file into a Web page by using the <IMG> tag. As you may expect, the position of the embedded image is determined by the position of the <IMG> statement in the HTML file. For example, if you define a push button, an embedded image, and a set of radio buttons, in that order, that's the order in which they appear on your Web page.

Tag Syntax for <IMG>	*Explanation*
<IMG	Opening <IMG> tag
NAME="imageName"	Name of image for internal coding purposes
SRC="location"	URL of image to load
[LOWSRC="location"]	URL of alternative low-resolution version of the image
[HEIGHT="pixels" | "value"%]	Height of image, in pixels or as a percentage of window height
[WIDTH="pixels" | "value"%]	Width of image, in pixels or as a percentage of window height
[HSPACE="pixels"]	Horizontal space between left and right sides of the image, and the left and right edges of the window, in pixels
[VSPACE="pixels"]	Vertical space between top and bottom of image and top and bottom edges of window, in pixels
[BORDER="pixels"]	Width of the image's border, if any, in pixels
[ALIGN="position"]	Specifies alignment of image
[ISMAP]	Whether the image is a server-side map
[USEMAP="location#mapName"]	Whether the image is a client-side map
[onAbort="handlerText"]	Code to execute when a user aborts an image load
[onError="handlerText"]	Code to execute when an error occurs on image load
[onLoad="handlerText"]>	Code to execute on image load

Most of the attributes are optional; only a few are strictly necessary, as you can see in the following example:

```
<IMG NAME="dogImage"
SRC="images/dalmation.gif"
ALIGN="MIDDLE">
```

See also Part IX for ideas on cool ways to adorn your Web pages with the ⟨IMG⟩ tag and other HTML multimedia morsels.

HTML comment: <!- . . . ->

Try to strike a balance between over-commenting and not adding enough comments to your code. Over-commenting can actually make your code harder to read; on the other hand, not adding any comments at all makes other HTML or JavaScript authors have to guess what your code is doing (and why the coding is doing it!).

```
<HTML>
. . .
<!- This HTML file was created by Juan Valdez,
    01/01/97
->
. . .
</HTML>
```

Two types of comments exist: HTML comments, which are demonstrated in the preceding code, and JavaScript comments, which look like this: // or /* */. These comments are *not* interchangeable. If you try to use an HTML comment inside a JavaScript script, you get an error. If you try to use a JavaScript comment inside an HTML tag, your JavaScript comment shows up on the Web page!

For a good example of proper comment usage, *see also* "Getting Started with a Bare-Bones HTML Template," in Part IX, or the "Comments" section in Part II.

Frame: <FRAMESET> . . . <FRAME> . . . </FRAMESET>

A *frame* is a special kind of window. You can have several frames per "regular" window, and a user can scroll each frame independently. Each frame can also be associated with a separate URL. What fun! What possibilities! (And — potentially — what confusion!)

To create a frame in HTML, use these tags:
⟨FRAMESET⟩...⟨FRAME⟩...⟨/FRAMESET⟩

To access that frame in JavaScript, use this identifier: frames[0]

In the preceding JavaScript identifier, 0 is a number representing the order in which the frame was defined in the HTML code. The first frame is represented by 0; the second, by 1; the third, by 2; and so on.

Tag Syntax for a Frame	Explanation
`<FRAMESET`	Opening `<FRAMESET>` tag (group of frames)
`ROWS="rowHeightList"`	Comma-separated list of values for row height
`COLS="columnWidthList"`	Comma-separated list of values for column width
`[onBlur="handlerText"]`	Code to invoke when window is blurred (optional)
`[onFocus="handlerText"]`	Code to invoke when window receives focus (optional)
`[onLoad="handlerText"]`	Code to invoke when window is loaded (optional)
`[onUnload="handlerText"]>`	Code to invoke when window is unloaded (optional)
`[<FRAME`	Single `<FRAME>` tag (optional but recommended)
`SRC="locationOrURL"`	URL of the document that appears in this frame
`NAME="frameName">]`	Internal name of frame (for coding purposes)
`</FRAMESET>`	Closing `</FRAMESET>` tag

Here's an example of code that defines two frames:

```
<HTML>
<HEAD><TITLE>Frames Example</TITLE></HEAD>
<FRAMESET ROWS="50%,50%" COLS="40%,60%">
<FRAME SRC="framcon1.html" NAME="frame1">
<FRAME SRC="framcon2.html" NAME="frame2">
</FRAMESET>
</HTML>
```

Hypertext anchor: <A> . . . </A>

An *anchor* is a piece of text that uniquely identifies a spot on a Web page. After you define an anchor, you (or any other HTML author) can link to it.

To define an anchor in HTML, use this tag pair: `<A>...</A>`

To access that anchor in JavaScript, use this identifier: `document.links[0]`

In the preceding JavaScript identifier, 0 is a number representing the order in which the anchor was defined in the HTML code. The first anchor is represented by 0; the second, by 1; the third, by 2; and so on.

You may notice that the ⟨A⟩...⟨/A⟩ tag pair is used for both anchors and links. If you want, you can use one ⟨A⟩...⟨/A⟩ tag pair to define a single piece of text that's both a link *and* an anchor.

Tag Syntax for an Anchor	Explanation
⟨A	Opening ⟨A⟩ tag
NAME="anchorName"⟩	Name of anchor to which the links refers
anchorText	Text to display at the anchor site
⟨/A⟩	Closing ⟨/A⟩ tag

Here's a down-and-dirty anchor definition:

⟨A NAME="TOC"⟩Table of Contents⟨/A⟩

Hypertext link: ⟨A⟩ ... ⟨/A⟩

Hypertext links (or just plain *links*) are at the heart of the Web's usefulness. You can use links to connect and organize multiple pages of your own, to connect your pages with other Web pages, or both. Technically, a *link* is a piece of text (or an image) that loads another Web page when you click on it. (A link sometimes loads a specific spot, or *anchor,* on the other Web page.)

To define a hypertext link in HTML, use this tag pair: ⟨A⟩...⟨/A⟩

To access that link in JavaScript, use this identifier:
document.links[0]

In the preceding JavaScript identifier, 0 is a number representing the order in which the link was defined in the HTML code. The first link is represented by 0; the second, by 1; the third, by 2; and so on.

Tag Syntax for a Link	Explanation
⟨A	Opening ⟨A⟩ tag
HREF="locationOrURL[#anchor]"	URL and (if appropriate) anchor to link to
[TARGET="windowName"]	Window to load linked page into (optional)
[onClick="handlerText"]	Code to invoke when a user clicks the link (optional)
[onMouseOut="handlerText"]	Code to invoke when mouse moves off the link (optional)
[onMouseOver="handlerText"]⟩	Code to invoke when mouse moves across the link (optional)
linkText	Text to display at link site
⟨/A⟩	Closing ⟨/A⟩ tag

Many of the link's attributes are optional. You can use them all if you're feeling frisky, but the following is a good example of all that's really necessary to get the job done:

```
<A HREF="http://www.dummies.com"> Link to the IDG
    Dummies Press Web Site </A>
```

When you move your mouse pointer over the link, the value specified for the HREF attribute (in this case, it's "http://www.dummies.com") appears in the status line at the bottom of the browser. You don't have to do anything special for this value to appear — the HTML interpreter does it for you automatically.

Inserting Interactive Form Elements: <INPUT>

To define an interactive input element in HTML, use this tag:
`<INPUT NAME="myInputElement"...>`

To access that element in JavaScript, use this identifier:
`document.myForm.myInputElement`

All the elements in this section are form elements and so must be defined between the <FORM>...</FORM> tags.

The interactive elements that you can create in JavaScript are actually HTML elements, with one very important difference: JavaScript lets you add event handlers (onClick, onChange, onBlur, and so on) to elements so that the elements can respond to user interaction (*see also* Part VI). You can make several different types of input elements interactive with JavaScript:

Input Element	Explanation
TYPE="button"	A customizable push button
TYPE="checkbox"	Grouped check boxes (which allow multiple selections)
TYPE="file"	A control that lets users browse and choose files
TYPE="hidden"	A text element that users can't see
TYPE="password"	A text element that displays characters as asterisks
TYPE="radio"	Grouped radio buttons (which restrict users to one selection)
TYPE="reset"	Predefined button to reset form values
<SELECT>	Configurable (single or multiple selection) list box
TYPE="submit"	Predefined button to submit form values
TYPE="text"	Single line text input field
<TEXTAREA>	Multiple line text input field

The `<SELECT>` and `<TEXTAREA>` elements are input elements, too, but they're defined a little differently than the others. (Go figure.) Instead of identifying values for the `TYPE` attribute of the `<INPUT>` tag, they have tags all their own:

```
<SELECT>...</SELECT>
<TEXTAREA>...</TEXTAREA>
```

Button

A button is a clickable push button on an HTML form.

Tag Syntax for a Button	Explanation
`<INPUT`	Single `<INPUT>` tag
`TYPE="button"`	Specifies the kind of input control (button)
`NAME="buttonName"`	Internal name of button (for coding purposes)
`VALUE="buttonText"`	Text to display on face of button
`[onClick="handlerText"]>`	Code to invoke when a user clicks the button

Here's a real-life example:

```
<INPUT TYPE="button" NAME="infoButton" VALUE="Click
    Here for Info" onClick="displayInfo()">
```

Check box

A check box is a toggle switch control. When users click a check box, they either check it (turn it on) or uncheck it (turn it off).

Tag Syntax for a Check Box	Explanation
`<INPUT`	Single `<INPUT>` tag
`TYPE="checkbox"`	Specifies the type of control (check box)
`NAME="checkboxName"`	Internal name of check box (for coding purposes)
`VALUE="checkboxValue"`	Value returned to the server when the form is submitted
`[CHECKED]`	Specifies initial display marked as checked (optional)
`[onClick="handlerText"]>`	Code to invoke when check box is clicked (optional)
`textToDisplay`	Descriptive text to display next to check box

Here's how you might go about creating a check box:

```
<INPUT TYPE="checkbox" NAME="classicalCheckbox"
    VALUE="checkedClassical"
    onClick="showClassicalTitles()"> Click here if
    you like classical music.
```

fileUpload

A fileUpload element allows users to browse the file directories on their own machine and choose a file. Within a JavaScript script you can access the name of the chosen file with the `fileUploadName.value`, which you can then use however you see fit.

The fileUpload element is available only for Netscape Navigator 3.0 at the time of this writing.

Tag Syntax for fileUpload	Explanation
`<INPUT`	Single `<INPUT>` tag
`TYPE="file"`	Specifies the type of element (file)
`NAME="fileUploadName">`	Specifies the name of the element

Here's what the definition of a fileUpload element looks like:

```
<INPUT TYPE="file" NAME="myFileUpload">
```

Hidden

A *hidden* element is an input text field that doesn't appear on-screen. Hidden elements are usually used to store programmer-calculated values (behind-the-scenes program stuff) that get sent to the server when the user submits a form.

Tag Syntax for a Hidden Element	Explanation
`<INPUT`	Single `<INPUT>` tag
`TYPE="hidden"`	Specifies the type of element (hidden)
`NAME="hiddenName"`	Internal name of hidden element (used in coding)
`[VALUE="textValue"]>`	Initial value of hidden object (optional)

Here's a garden-variety definition for a hidden element:

```
<INPUT TYPE="hidden" NAME="secretTextField">
```

Password

A *password* object is a special text input field that displays asterisks on the screen (in place of the characters that the user actually types).

Tag Syntax for a Password	Explanation
`<INPUT`	Single `<INPUT>` tag
`TYPE="password"`	Specifies the type of element (password)
`NAME="passwordName"`	Internal name of password (for coding purposes)
`SIZE=integer`	Number of characters to display initially
`[VALUE="textValue"]>`	Initial value of password (optional)

Take a look at this sample password definition:

```
<INPUT TYPE="password" NAME="userPassword" SIZE=15
    VALUE="secret!">
```

Radio button

A *radio button* is a toggle switch control, as is a check box. Unlike a check box, however, radio buttons are most often grouped in sets, which allow users to select a *single* option from a list.

Tag Syntax for a Radio Button	Explanation
`<INPUT`	Single `<INPUT>` tag
`TYPE="radio"`	Specifies the kind of element (radio)
`NAME="radioName"`	Internal name of radio button (for coding purposes)
`VALUE="radioValue"`	Specifies a value to be returned to the server
`[CHECKED]`	Specifies that this button is initially selected (optional)
`[onClick="handlerText"]>`	Code to invoke when user clicks on radio button (optional)
`textToDisplay`	Descriptive text

The following code shows a common way to define a set of radio buttons. Notice how the value for the NAME attribute is the same (timeChoice) for every radio button? Because all three radio buttons share one name (and only one value can be associated with one name at a time), the user is effectively restricted to selecting only one radio button from the entire group.

```
What's your favorite time of day?
<INPUT TYPE="radio" NAME="timeChoice"
    VALUE="morningSelected" CHECKED
onClick="showValues(0)"> Morning

<INPUT TYPE="radio" NAME="timeChoice"
    VALUE="afternoonSelected"
onClick="showValues(1)"> Afternoon

<INPUT TYPE="radio" NAME="timeChoice"
    VALUE="eveningSelected"
onClick="showValues(2)"> Evening
```

Reset

A *reset* object is a special kind of button. When a user clicks on the reset button, all the user-input values in a form are cleared and reset to their initial (default) values.

Tag Syntax for a Reset Button	Explanation
`<INPUT`	Single `<INPUT>` tag
`TYPE="reset"`	Specifies type of control (reset)
`NAME="resetName"`	Internal name of control (for coding purposes)
`VALUE="buttonText"`	Text to display on face of reset button
`[onClick="handlerText"]>`	Code to invoke when a user clicks the button (optional)

Here's an example of how to add a reset button to your form:

```
<INPUT TYPE="reset" NAME="resetButton" VALUE="Reset
    Form Now" onClick="reinitializeFormulas()">
```

Select

The `<SELECT>` element is used to display both a single-selection list and a scrolling multiple-selection list box (depending on whether you specify the `MULTIPLE` attribute).

The `<SELECT>` element is one of the two input elements (`<TEXTAREA>` is the other) that don't follow the standard convention of specifying the element as the value for the `<INPUT>` tag's `TYPE` attribute. Unlike the other interactive objects that you put in an HTML document by using the `<INPUT>` tag and an attribute, you simply use the `<SELECT>` tag to put a list box in your Web page, as you can see in the following table.

Tag Syntax for a Select List Box	Explanation
`<SELECT`	Opening `<SELECT>` tag
`NAME="selectName"`	Internal name of control (for coding purposes)
`[SIZE=integer]`	Number of options visible (optional; default is 1)
`[MULTIPLE]`	Specifies multiple-selection scrolling box (optional)
`[onBlur="handlerText"]`	Code to invoke when focus is lost (the user clicks elsewhere)
`[onChange="handlerText"]`	Code to invoke when value changes and focus is lost
`[onFocus="handlerText"]>`	Code to invoke when focus is received (user clicks on element)
`<OPTION`	Specifies a selection item
`[VALUE="optionValue"]`	Value returned to server when user submits a form
`[SELECTED]>`	Specifies that this option is selected by default
`textToDisplay`	Descriptive text to display next to option
`</SELECT>`	Closing `</SELECT>` tag

You can repeat the `OPTION` tag (and its associated attributes) as needed, once for each option that you provide.

Because adding a list box to a Web page entails working not only with the usual associated attributes you've come to expect, but an additional tag, too (the `<OPTION>` tag), it can be a little confusing at first. Here's a short, to-the-point example to help you get started:

```
<SELECT NAME="favoriteMusic" SIZE=3 MULTIPLE
    onBlur="displayResult(this)">

<OPTION VALUE="popChosen" SELECTED> pop
<OPTION VALUE="rockChosen" > rock
<OPTION VALUE="dogsChosen" > dogs barking Jingle
    Bells
<OPTION VALUE="rapChosen" > rap
<OPTION VALUE="showChosen" > show tunes
<OPTION VALUE="africanChosen" > African classical

</SELECT>
```

Submit

A *Submit* element is a special kind of button that submits (or sends) values from a form to a server (specifically, to a particular CGI program on a particular server that you define as part of the <FORM>...</FORM> tag pair). The submit button works in tandem with the ACTION attribute of the <FORM>...</FORM> tag pair. You can find more information about submitting form values to a CGI server in "Specifying Useful Web Page Features," later in this part.

Tag Syntax for a Submit Button	Explanation
<INPUT	Single <INPUT> tag
TYPE="submit"	Specifies kind of control (submit)
NAME="submitName"	Internal name of submit button (for coding purposes)
VALUE="submitText"	Text to display on face of submit button
[onClick="handlerText"]>	Code to invoke when user clicks submit button (technically optional, but practically necessary!)

Here's a practical example:

```
<INPUT TYPE="submit" NAME="submitButton"
VALUE="Submit Form" onClick="verifyInput()">
```

Text

The *text* element is a single-line input field.

Tag Syntax for a Text Element	Explanation
<INPUT	Single <INPUT> tag
TYPE="text"	Specifies the kind of control (text)
NAME="textName"	Internal name of the text field (for coding purposes)
VALUE="textValue"	Specifies initial value of text field
SIZE=integer	Number of characters to display before scrolling
[onBlur="handlerText"]	Code to invoke when a user clicks elsewhere and focus is lost (optional)
[onChange="handlerText"]	Code to invoke when value changes *and* focus is lost (optional)

(continued)

Tag Syntax for a Text Element	Explanation
[onFocus="handlerText"]	Code to invoke when user clicks on the element and focus is received (optional)
[onSelect="handlerText"]>	Code to invoke when text in the field is highlighted (optional)

Here's a simple illustration of the text element in action:

```
<INPUT TYPE="text" NAME="lastName" VALUE="Your name
    here"
SIZE=30 onChange="validate()">
```

Textarea

A <TEXTAREA> element is just like a text element, except that instead of defining one scrolling input line, the <TEXTAREA> element defines a multiline scroll box so that users can type in whole reams of text. Like <SELECT>, <TEXTAREA> doesn't follow the standard input element convention of specifying the element as the value for the <INPUT> tag's TYPE attribute. Instead, the <INPUT> tag is replaced in this case by the <TEXTAREA> tag, as shown in the following table.

Tag Syntax for a Textarea Element	Explanation
<TEXTAREA	Opening <TEXTAREA> tag
NAME="textareaName"	Internal name of textarea object (for coding)
ROWS=integer	Number of rows to display
COLS=integer	Number of columns to display
[onBlur="handlerText"]	Code to invoke when textarea loses focus (optional)
[onChange="handlerText"]	Code to invoke when value changes and focus is lost (optional)
[onFocus="handlerText"]	Code to invoke when focus is received (optional)
[onSelect="handlerText"]>	Code to invoke when text is highlighted (optional)
textToDisplay	Initial text to display inside scroll box
</TEXTAREA>	Closing </TEXTAREA> tag

Here's a garden-variety textarea example for you to see:

```
<TEXTAREA NAME="directions" ROWS=4 COLS=60
onBlur="validate()" onChange="display()"
onFocus="welcome()" onSelect="changeMode()">
This is default text. You can type right over it,
add to it, cut it, paste it, or copy it.
</TEXTAREA>
```

Inserting a Java Applet: <APPLET> . . . </APPLET>

A *Java applet* is a special little software program specifically designed to live inside a Web page.

JavaScript For Dummies, by yours truly, contains a whole chapter dedicated to Java and JavaScript-to-Java interaction. Also check out *Java For Dummies,* by Aaron Walsh, for more low-down on Java applets.

To embed a Java applet in your Web page, use this tag pair:
`<APPLET>...</APPLET>`

To access a Java applet in JavaScript, use this identifier:
`document.applets[0]`

In the preceding JavaScript identifier, 0 is a number representing the order in which the applet was defined in the HTML code. The first applet you define is represented by 0; the second, by 1; the third, by 2; and so forth.

When you embed a Java applet in your HTML code, you need to know a little bit about that applet. For example, some applets require *parameters,* which are values that you send an applet when you embed it. (Because applet function is restricted only by the Java programmer's imagination, the parameters you may be required to supply are equally diverse.) If you want to embed an applet that requires parameters, you have to include those parameters in your `<APPLET>...</APPLET>` definition. Two ways exist to find out what any given applet requires so that you can embed it in your Web page:

   ✦ Surf the Web until you find an example of how someone else embedded the applet and follow that example. (Typically, this is how you find out about applets in the first place.)

   ✦ E-mail the applet programmer directly and ask for instructions.

Tag Syntax to Embed a Java Applet	Explanation
`<APPLET`	Beginning `<APPLET>` tag
`CODE="classFileName"`	File name of the applet to load (`*.class`)
`HEIGHT=height`	Height of the applet, in pixels
`WIDTH=width`	Width of the applet, in pixels
`[MAYSCRIPT]`	If specified, this attribute permits the applet to access JavaScript values (optional)
`[NAME="appletName"]`	Name of applet for internal coding purposes (optional but recommended)
`[CODEBASE="classFileDirectory"]`	Directory where classFileName is located (optional but recommended)
`[ALT="alternateText"]`	Text to display in place of applet (for browsers that don't support Java; optional)
`[ALIGN="position"]`	Specifies alignment of applet on HTML page (optional)
`[HSPACE=numberOfPixels]`	Horizontal margin of applet, in pixels (optional)
`[VSPACE=numberOfPixels]/`	Vertical margin for applet, in pixels (optional)
You can repeat the following optional section as many times as necessary:	
`[<PARAM`	Opening `<PARAM>` tag
`NAME="parameterName"`	Name of parameter to pass to applet
`VALUE="parameterValue">]`	Value to pass to applet
`[</PARAM>]`	Closing `<PARAM>` tag
`</APPLET>`	Ending `</APPLET>` tag

The value for `ALIGN` can be any of the following string values: `LEFT`, `RIGHT`, `TOP`, `ABSMIDDLE`, `ABSBOTTOM`, `TEXTTOP`, `MIDDLE`, `BASELINE`, or `BOTTOM`.

Here's an example of code that embeds an applet that doesn't require any parameters. (It actually works, if you want to try it out for yourself; if you do, you'll see a handful of animated, multicolored bubbles drift lazily from the bottom of the applet space up to the top.)

```
<APPLET NAME="BubbleApplet"
CODE="Bubbles.class"
CODEBASE="http://java.sun.com/applets/applets/
    Bubbles"
WIDTH=500 HEIGHT=500>
</APPLET>
```

Mapping an Area: <MAP>...<AREA>... </MAP>

An area is like a big, thick link: An area describes a space on your page, which you can shape and size as you want and which responds to user events. Areas are used to create what are called *clickable maps;* as you move your mouse around on an image, the link (or URL) that appears in your Web browser's status line changes.

To embed an area in your Web page, use this tag pair:
<MAP>...<AREA>...</MAP>

To access that area in JavaScript, use this identifier:
document.links[0]

No, the preceding line isn't a typo! Areas are stored in the links array, right along with regular, "skinny" links.

Tag Syntax to Embed an Area	Explanation
<MAP	Opening <MAP> tag (you need to define a map to define an area)
NAME="mapName">	Name of map for internal coding purposes
<AREA	Opening <AREA> tag
NAME="areaName"	Name of area for internal coding purposes
COORDS="x1, y1, x2, y2"	Coordinates of the image map, in integers
HREF="location"	URL of document to load when user clicks on an area, or "javascript:*functionName()*"
[SHAPE="shape"]	Shape of the map (see the Tip that follows the table)
[TARGET="windowName"]	Window to load link into when a user clicks on an area
[onMouseOut="handlerText"]	Code to execute when mouse pointer moves out of area
[onMouseOver="handlerText"]	Code to execute when mouse pointer is dragged across area
</MAP>	Closing </MAP> tag

Here's a sample area definition:

```
<MAP NAME="thistleMap">

<AREA NAME="topThistle" COORDS="0,0,228,318"
    HREF="javascript:void(0)"
onMouseOver="self.status='That mouse pointer sure
    feels nice'; return true"
onMouseOut="self.status='Thanks for visiting; come
    again!'; return true">
</MAP>
```

The preceding code snippet creates a map that matches the boundaries of a picture. (The picture in this case happens to be of bright pink thistles, which is why the name of the map is `thistleMap`.) When a user moves the cursor onto the picture/map, the text `'That mouse pointer sure feels nice'` appears in the status bar. When a user drags the cursor away from the picture/map so that the cursor rests somewhere else on the screen, the text in the status bar changes to `"Thanks for visiting; come again!"`

The value for `SHAPE` can be any of the following strings: `"rect"`, `"poly"`, `"circle"`, or `"default"`. If you don't define any value for the `SHAPE` attribute, the shape defaults to `"rect"`.

Plugging in a Plug-in: <EMBED>... </EMBED>

Netscape plug-ins are software components that "plug in" to Netscape Navigator to extend its capabilities.

To embed a plug-in into your Web page, use this tag pair:
`<EMBED>...</EMBED>`

To access that plug-in in JavaScript, use this identifier:
`navigator.plugins[0]`

In the preceding JavaScript identifier, 0 is a number representing the order the plug-in was embedded in your HTML code. The first plug-in you embed is represented by 0; the second, by 1; the third, by 2; and so forth.

You define the `plugin` object by using the `<EMBED>` tag. The output of the plug-in that you embed appears in the same space on your form where the `plugin` object appears.

Tag Syntax to Embed a Plug-In	Explanation
`<EMBED`	Opening `<EMBED>` tag
`SRC="source"`	URL containing the source of the plug-in
`NAME="embedName"`	Name of embedded plug-in object (for internal coding purposes)
`HEIGHT=height`	Height of embedded plug-in, in pixels
`WIDTH=width>`	Width of embedded plug-in, in pixels
You can repeat the following optional section as many times as necessary:	
`[<PARAM`	Opening `<PARAM>` tag
`NAME="parameterName"`	Name of parameter (argument) to pass to plug-in
`VALUE="parameterValue">]`	Value of parameter (argument) to pass to plug-in
`[</PARAM>]`	Closing `</PARAM>` tag
`</EMBED>`	Closing `</EMBED>` tag

If you're unfamiliar with plug-ins — what they are, how they work, and why the heck you'd ever want to embed one in your Web page — you may want to take a look at the following URL which lists a treasure trove of plug-ins for sale:

```
http://home.netscape.com/comprod/
    development_partners/plugin_api/
    plugin_design.html
```

Here's an example that you can try out for yourself. This code uses the Adobe Acrobat plug-in to display a .pdf file, which is a file with a fancy graphic display format.

```
<EMBED NAME="myEmbed" SRC="http://
    ecco.bsee.swin.edu.au/text/adobe/PDFs/
    AcroCD.pdf"
WIDTH=450 HEIGHT=450>
</EMBED>
```

Specifying Useful Web Page Features

This section contains examples of useful things you may want to configure your Web pages to do:

✦ Call a CGI program

✦ Display a title

CGI program to call on submit: <FORM> . . . </FORM>

When a user clicks on a submit push button in a form, all the values contained in that form are sent automatically to a Common Gateway Interface (CGI) program. You specify a particular CGI program as the value of the ACTION attribute of the <FORM> tag. If you don't specify a CGI program for the ACTION attribute, nothing happens when a user clicks on the submit push button, which is great for testing. In real life, though, if you're going to the trouble of adding a submit push button, you need to specify a value for the ACTION attribute, as shown in the following code:

```
<FORM
...
ACTION="http://www.madeup.com/cgi-bin/
    someCGIProgram">
...
</FORM>
```

Wait until your Web page is behaving nicely before you specify a CGI program to which you want to submit your form data. That way, you can test and refine your JavaScript statements first (before you complicate matters by introducing the CGI program).

Title for your Web page: <TITLE>. . .</TITLE>

Titles play an important part in communicating your message (whatever that may be) to your users. Not only are the words in your title used by many Web-searching programs, but when users save a reference to your Web page (sometimes called *bookmarking*), your title is what appears on their list of saved references. For these reasons alone it's worth spending a little time on wording your title.

Notice in the following example that the <TITLE>...</TITLE> tags are placed between the <HEAD>...</HEAD> tags.

```
<HTML>
<HEAD>
<TITLE>
Dave's Retail Catalogue of Restored Antique Wood-
    Burning Stoves
</TITLE>
</HEAD>
</HTML>
```

Although you're not required to place the title between the <HEAD> tags (the title will *still* appear if you place the <TITLE>...</TITLE> tags after the <HEAD>...</HEAD> tags), the example shows the standard style used by the Web-savvy crowd.

Part II

JavaScript Basics

This part is like a JavaScript grammar book, dictionary, and thesaurus — all rolled into one. In this part, you find the nuts-and-bolts mechanics of writing JavaScript statements — from syntax to special keywords, from declaring variables to defining and calling functions. You also find an overview of all the objects you can work with in JavaScript. (For a detailed description of each object in the overview, *see also* Part III.)

In this part . . .

✔ **Understanding the security issues associated with JavaScript scripts**

✔ **Becoming familiar with the JavaScript object model**

✔ **Unraveling JavaScript syntax and expressions**

About JavaScript Security

Because JavaScript runs on the client computer, its ability to cause security breaches is fairly limited. Security issues are more of a concern when client/server communication is involved, and this type of communication isn't included in JavaScript's bag of tricks.

As of this writing, only one minor problem has been widely publicized, and that's the ability of a mischievous JavaScripter to set up a harmless-looking button that sends an e-mail message (complete with your e-mail address) to the mischief-maker, without your knowledge.

Fortunately, this problem only rears its ugly head with the Netscape Navigator 3.0 Web browser, and it's completely preventable. From the Navigator browser main window, all you have to do is choose Options⇨Network Preferences⇨Protocols. Then, in the Show an Alert Before box, click the check box labeled Submitting a Form by Email, and the problem is solved: Any time that your Web browser attempts to send e-mail, an alert window notifies you and gives you the opportunity to cancel the proceedings.

Because developers tend to take security issues very seriously, expect each version of Netscape Navigator and Microsoft Internet Explorer to be more secure than its predecessor.

Web security is a hot topic these days — whenever information passes across the Internet, there's *always* an associated security hazard. CGI programs, plug-ins, Java applets, and cookies all present different security risks that you may want to be aware of. If you plan to integrate your JavaScript scripts with any of these elements (or just to find out more about staying secure on the Internet, in general), check out *Computer Security For Dummies,* by Peter Davis and Barry Lewis (published by IDG Books Worldwide, Inc.).

This Web site is devoted exclusively to JavaScript-related security issues:

```
http://ciac.llnl.gov/ciac/javasecure.html
```

Basics of the JavaScript Object Model

You can work with three main kinds of objects in JavaScript:

+ Built-in data types

+ Objects that make up a Web page

+ Utility objects

Read on for a quick rundown of each object type and the differences between them.

Built-in JavaScript data types

Numbers, *Boolean* values *(true* or *false)*, and strings (a bunch of characters surrounded by quotes, like "this") are such basic programming building blocks (called *data types*) that you don't even have to create special objects to use them in JavaScript. All you have to do is specify a numeric, Boolean, or string value, and the JavaScript interpreter takes care of the rest.

Look at the following examples to see what I mean:

Built-in Data Type	JavaScript Syntax
Boolean	`var loveWork = true`
null	`var middleInitial = null`
number	`var myAge = 29`
string	`var fullName = "Kris Kringle"`

In the preceding table, you create four different variables to hold four different values, each associated with a different data type. The first variable, `loveWork`, is assigned the Boolean value `true`; the second variable, `middleInitial`, is assigned the `null` value; the third variable, `myAge`, is assigned a number; and the fourth value, `fullName`, is assigned a string value. Taken together, the JavaScript interpreter reads these variables as, "Kris Kringle is age 29, has no middle initial, and loves his work."

The `null` data type means "nothing" (which is different from simply not assigning any value). The `null` data type is a valid value all on its own.

Hierarchy of JavaScript objects

You can think of the JavaScript object hierarchy as your favorite browser's object hierarchy, because you create these objects in HTML (a few are even created for you automatically by the browser itself) before JavaScript ever enters the picture. After the objects exist, JavaScript lets you examine them, change them, perform calculations based on them, and do pretty much whatever else your heart desires.

Notice in the following table that when one object is contained in another, that containment is reflected in the JavaScript syntax. For example, a button is defined in HTML as part of a form which, itself, is part of the overall HTML document. So if you want to access a button, you need to type this code:

`document.nameOfYourForm.nameOfYourButton`

Object	HTML Tag	JavaScript Syntax
window	none (it's a given)	window (optional)
document	`<HTML>...</HTML>`	document
anchor	`<A>...</A>`	document. *links[0]*
applet	`<APPLET>...</APPLET>`	document. *applets[0]*
area	`<MAP>...<AREA>...</MAP>`	document. *someArea*
form	`<FORM>...</FORM>`	document. *someForm*
button	`<INPUT TYPE=` `"button">`	document. *someForm.* *someButton*
checkbox	`<INPUT TYPE=` `"checkbox">`	document. *someForm.* *myCheckbox*
fileUpload	`<INPUT TYPE=` `"file">`	document. *someForm.* *myFileUpload*
hidden	`<INPUT TYPE=` `"hidden">`	document. *someForm.* *someHidden*
image	`<IMG>`	document. *someForm.* *someImage*
password	`<INPUT TYPE=` `"password">`	document. *someForm.* *somePassword*
radio	`<INPUT TYPE=` `"radio">`	document. *someForm.* *someRadio*
reset	`<INPUT TYPE=` `"reset">`	document. *someForm.* *someReset*
select	`<SELECT>...</SELECT>`	document. *someForm.* *someSelect*
submit	`<INPUT TYPE="submit">`	document. *someForm.* *someSubmit*
text	`<INPUT TYPE="text">`	document. *someForm.* *someText*

Object	HTML Tag	JavaScript Syntax

textarea	`<TEXTAREA>...`
	`</TEXTAREA>`
		`document.`
		`someForm.`
		`someTextarea`

link	`<A>...</A>`	`document.` `links[0]`
plugin	`<EMBED>...</EMBED>`	`document.` `embeds[0]`
frame	`<FRAMESET>...` `</FRAMESET>`	`frame`
history	none (it's a given)	`history`
location	none (it's a given)	`location`
navigator	none (it's a given)	`navigator`

See also Part I to find out about the individual HTML tags that create each object.

Both the `window` and the `frame` objects have associated aliases. (An *alias* is an alternative way of referring to an object and should be used if doing so makes your code easier to understand.)

You can refer to a `window` by any of the following identifiers: `parent` (if the window in question is the parent of the window containing the reference); `self` (if the window in question is the same window as the one containing the reference); or `top` (if the window in question is at the top of the window hierarchy containing the reference).

Similarly, a frame can be referred to by either `parent` or `self`.

Utility objects

Utility objects, unlike the objects that make up the JavaScript object hierarchy, don't represent any one piece of a Web page. As the following table shows, utility objects are just useful stand-alone utilities — arrays, date, functions — that you may want to use in your JavaScript statements.

Utility Object	JavaScript Syntax
Array	`var myPets = new Array` `("Spike", "Zeke", "Fluffy")`
Date	`var today = new Date()`

Function	`var salary = new Function`
	`("base", "commission",`
	`"return base + (base *`
	`commission))"`

(continued)

Utility Object	JavaScript Syntax
Math	`var randomNumber = Math.random()`
Option	`var blues = new Option("Blues music", "blues", true, true)`

An `Option` object isn't much use by itself; it's only meaningful when it's related to a `select` list box. Normally, you define options with HTML statements at the same time you define the list box itself. Alternatively, you can define them as shown with the `Option` utility object.

Basic Punctuation and Syntax

As programming languages go, JavaScript is pretty easy to learn. (I know, easy for me to say!) Just like English, the JavaScript language is made up of words and punctuation, which you, gentle JavaScripter, must combine to form meaningful statements. Between Part III, which describes all the JavaScript objects in detail, and this part, which describes all the JavaScript syntax and keywords, you have everything you need to write your very own scripts.

Some JavaScript interpreters are a little more forgiving than others, but no guarantee exists that future versions won't tighten the screws a bit. What that means is that, while bending the punctuation rules in this section may work for now (for example, you may be able to get away with leaving off a piece of punctuation here or there), it probably won't work in all browsers, or for very long (and long in Web years is about three months!). To be on the safe side, always follow the guidelines in this section.

If you are familiar with C or C++, you may immediately notice JavaScript's lack of a statement-ending semicolon. Punctuation *is* a little less complicated in JavaScript than it is in C or C++, but it's not foolproof! JavaScript still provides you the flexibility to make a couple of annoying punctuation errors — and this section helps you avoid them.

Nested quotes

You use quotes in JavaScript — both single quotes (') and double quotes (") — to surround string values. Why both kinds of quotes? Because you may run into a situation where you need to use two sets of quotes in a single JavaScript statement. If so, you need to use both single *and* double quotes and alternate them.

If you try to nest double quotes inside double quotes (or single quotes inside single quotes), you run into trouble. Here's an example:

```
onClick="alert('This is an example of correctly
    nested quotes.')"

onClick="alert("Warning! This statement will
    produce an error.")"

onClick='alert('Warning! This statement is wrong,
    too.')'
```

If you want a double quote to *appear* in a string, here's what you do: Precede the double quote with a backslash. (This action is called *escaping* the quote.) Here's what it looks like:

```
alert("Did you like the movie \"Phenomenon\"?")
```

Pairs

JavaScript scripts are typically rife with pairs — pairs of opening and closing tags and angle brackets (courtesy of HTML), pairs of parentheses, pairs of quotes, and pairs of curly braces. If you forget to add a closing bracket, brace, or whatever, the JavaScript interpreter complains. Sometimes the complaint takes the form of a syntax error; sometimes you get a goofy-looking page display.

Following are some examples of pair mismatching to look out for:

HTML/JavaScript Statement	Error
`<FORM NAME="myForm"`	Missing right angle bracket (>)
`<A HREF="http://www.tucows. com">Two Cows`	Missing closing tag (</A>)
`alert("Form processing complete."`	Missing parenthesis ())
`firstName = "Barney`	Missing quote (")
`if (name == "") { alert("Please enter your name.")`	Missing curly brace (})

Spelling and capitalization (case)

All the words you use in programming JavaScript must be spelled correctly. For example, if you create a variable called lastName and then try to display it on your Web page but misspell it as lastNam, you get an error. As close as these two words may appear to human eyes, they look nothing alike to the JavaScript interpreter.

Character case is just as important as correct spelling. For example, the JavaScript interpreter won't recognize the variable named `lastName` if you type it `LastName`.

Top-down

The JavaScript interpreter reads from top to bottom, left to right. So, before you can use something, that something must first be defined. Case in point: In order to *call* (or use) a function, you must first define that function in an earlier statement. Likewise, if you want to access a variable, you must declare that variable first.

Comments (/*. . .*/ and //)

Comments aren't processed at all by the JavaScript interpreter; they're ignored. A comment's purpose is to give script authors a free-form way to communicate with themselves (you'd be surprised how quickly you forget why you did something the way you did it!) and any other humans who read their scripts.

Two different kinds of JavaScript comments exist. Either can appear anywhere in your script, as many times as you want.

You create a single-line comment by typing a double slash (//) at the beginning of the line, followed by your comment, like this:

```
// This is a single-line comment.
```

Create a multiple-line comment by beginning a line with /* and ending your comment with */, like so:

```
/* This comment can span multiple lines. Always
   remember to close it off, though; if you for-
   get, you'll get weird errors when you try to
   display your script. */
```

Nesting multiple-line comments is a bad idea. A block of code like the following can cause grief because the interpreter ignores the second /* when it gets to the first */:

```
/* Blocking out this section for testing pur-
   poses...
       /* Here is a comment. */
*/
```

Conditional Expressions: if ... else

The if...else expression is called a *conditional* expression because you use it to test whether a certain condition is true. A condition can be a variable, a statement, or an expression — anything at all that can be resolved by the JavaScript interpreter to a simple true or false answer.

If the condition is *true,* the interpreter executes all the statements between curly braces that follow the if clause. If the condition is *false,* the interpreter executes all the statements between curly braces that follow the else clause. Here's the generic description of how to use if...else:

```
if (condition) {
    statements
}
[ else {
    statements
}]
```

The square brackets around the else clause mean that the else clause is optional — it's possible to code just the if clause, if you want. And no rule says that an if...else expression can't have other statements nested inside of it, either (many do). Just remember to include the curly braces as shown for each if...else. There's no leeway here; they have to be curly braces, not parentheses, and they have to come in pairs, just like in the following example:

```
if (numberOrdered <= 100) {
    //calculate the order at retail cost
    calculateTotal(19.95)
}
else {
    // calculate the order at wholesale cost
    calculateTotal(11.00)
}
```

Loops

Loops are common programming constructs that you can use to perform a single task many times, in as compact a way as possible. JavaScript contains two basic kinds of loops: for and while. Both types of loops are explained in the following sections, along with some other keywords that you can use with for and while to create concise, powerful loops.

break

The break keyword must be used inside of a loop (your loop choices are for, for...in, and while). When the JavaScript interpreter encounters a break statement, it breaks out of the loop entirely and starts interpreting again at the first line following the loop. For example:

```
for (var i = 1; i<= 20; i++) {
    . . .
    if (i == 13) {   // Only go up to 12
        break
    }
    document.writeln(i)
}
// this is where the interpreter will pick up again
// after the break
```

Here's how the output will look:

```
1 2 3 4 5 6 7 8 9 10 11 12
```

continue

Like break, continue can be used inside for, for...in, or while loops. When the JavaScript interpreter encounters a continue statement, it stops what it's doing and hops back up to the beginning of the loop to continue as normal. The following example may make it clearer:

```
for (var i = 1; i<= 20; i++) {
    if (i == 13) {   // Superstitious! Don't print
    #13
        continue
    }
    document.writeln(i)
}
```

The following output shows you exactly how continue works. You may want to compare the following output to the output generated by break:

```
1 2 3 4 5 6 7 8 9 10 11 12 14 15 16 17 18 19 20
```

In the output generated by continue, you can see that the number 13 is skipped — but then the loop continues and prints out the numbers 14 through 20 (unlike the break command, which stops the loop dead in its tracks after printing the number 12).

 The continue keyword is useful for handling exceptions to a rule. For example, you may want to process all the items in a group the same way except for one or two special cases.

for

The `for` loop comes straight from the C language — and since C is famous for its terseness, it won't come as a shock to you that in the wrong hands, `for` loops can be positively Byzantine.

First, have a look at the generic form:

```
for ([initial expression]; [condition]; [update
    expression]) {
    statements
}
```

The preceding syntax introduces three terms that may be new to you:

+ **Initial expression:** Think of the *initial expression* as the starting point — a snapshot of how things look right before the interpreter hops into the loop and gets down to business.

+ **Condition:** The *condition* is the JavaScript expression to be tested each time the interpreter takes a pass around the loop.

+ **Update expression:** If the condition tests true, the JavaScript interpreter performs the *update expression* before looping around to test the condition again.

Here's a short example that should help make the workings of the `for` loop crystal clear:

```
for (var i = 1; i <= 10; i++) {
    document.writeln(i)
}
```

The following steps describe what happens in the preceding `for` loop:

1. The variable i is set equal to 1.

2. The JavaScript interpreter checks to see whether i is less than or equal to 10.

3. i is less than or equal to 10, so the body of the loop executes.

4. i is written to the screen (this one action, `document.writeln(i)`, forms the entire body of the loop).

5. The JavaScript interpreter adds 1 to i; now i is 2.

6. The JavaScript interpreter checks to see whether i is less than or equal to 10.

7. i is less than or equal to 10, so the body of the loop executes.

8. i is written to the screen via the `document.writeln` method (again, this one action comprises the entire loop body).

9. The JavaScript interpreter adds 1 to i; now i is 3.

10. Start again at Step 6.

See the pattern? The interpreter begins at the top of the loop and performs the body of the loop once for each time that the loop condition is true.

for . . . in

If you like the for loop, you'll love for...in. The two are very similar, but unlike for, you use the for...in loop exclusively for looping, or *iterating,* through all the properties of an object, like so:

```
for (var in object) {
    statements
}
```

To elaborate, here's a function that loops through all the properties of a given object. As the function loops through, it builds a string (called result) containing the name and value of each property it finds.

```
function displayProperties(inputObject,
    inputObjectName){
    var result = ""
    for (var eachProperty in inputObject) {
        result + = inputObjectName
                + "."
                + eachProperty
                + " = "
                + inputObject[eachProperty]
                + "<BR>"
    }
    result + = "<HR>"
    return result
}
```

Here's what the output for the preceding code snippet might look like if the text input element aTextField were passed into the loop:

```
document.myForm.aTextField.type = text
document.myForm.aTextField.name = aTextField
document.myForm.aTextField.form = [object Form]
document.myForm.aTextField.value = My dog has
    fleas.
document.myForm.aTextField.defaultValue = null
```

while

The while loop is similar to the for loop. First you set up a condition, and *while* that condition is true, the JavaScript interpreter executes the statements in the body of the loop. If the condition is *never* true, the statements never execute; if the condition is *always* true, well, let's just say that those statements will execute for a long, long, long, long time. Obviously, then, you want to make sure that one of the statements in the body of your `while` loop changes the `while` condition in some way so that it stops being true at some point.

First, the generic syntax:

```
while (condition) {
    statements
}
```

Now here's an example of `while` in action:

```
while (totalInventory > numberPurchased) {
    totalInventory = totalInventory -
    numberPurchased
    numberSales++
}
```

Operators

Operators are kind of like conjunctions in English: You use operators to join multiple phrases together to form expressions. The operators you're familiar with in everyday life include the plus sign (+) and the minus sign (–). JavaScript provides you with a lot more operators, however, as you can see in the following sections.

Assignment operators

Assignment operators let you assign values to variables. Besides being able to make a straight one-to-one assignment, though, you can also use some of them as a kind of shorthand to bump up a value based on another value. The following table describes how each operator works:

Operator	Meaning	Example (x = 10, y = 15 each time)
x = y	The value of y is assigned to x	x = 15
x += y	x = x + y (addition)	x = 25
x -= y	x = x – y (subtraction)	x = –5
x *= y	x = x * y (multiplication)	x = 150
x /= y	x = x / y (division)	x = .6666666
x %= y	x = x % y (modulus)	x = 10

TIP

Here's how the modulus operator works: x %= y means that the interpreter tries to divide y into x evenly. The result is anything left over. In the preceding example, x is 10 and y is 15. 15 won't go into 10 evenly at all, so 10 is what's left over.

Comparison operators

When comparing two values or expressions for equality, you've got the following choices:

Operator	Example	Meaning
== (two equal signs)	x == y	x is equal to y
!=	x != y	x is not equal to y
<	x < y	x is less than y
>	x > y	x is greater than y
<=	x <= y	x is less than or equal to y
>=	x >= y	x is greater than or equal to y
? :	x = (y < 0) ? -y : y	If y is less than zero, assign −y to x; otherwise, assign y to x

WARNING

A common mistake that beginning programmers often make is using a singe equal sign in place of a double equal sign (and vice versa). JavaScript doesn't complain if you do this; after all, both (x == 6) and (x = 6) are legal expressions, and JavaScript has no way of knowing which expression you really want to state. The two examples are radically different, though, and interchanging them can wreak havoc on your logic. The first example *compares* 6 to x, and the second *assigns* 6 to x!

Logical operators

Logical operators work on logical values (also called Boolean values) and they also return Boolean values. A Boolean value can only be one of two things: It's either *true* or it's *false*. When you see two expressions separated by a logical operator, the JavaScript interpreter first computes (or *resolves*) the expressions to see whether each is true or false; then it computes the entire statement. If an expression resolves to a number *other than* zero, the expression is considered to be true; if the expression computes *to* zero, it's considered to be false. Check out the following table for examples of the logical operators available in JavaScript:

Operator	*Name*	*Example*	*Meaning*
&&	logical "and"	if (x == y && a != b)	If x is equal to y AND a is not equal to b
||	logical "or"	if (x < y || a < b)	If x is less than y OR a is less than b
!	not	if (!x)	If NOT x (that is, if x is false, or zero)

Mathematical operators

Mathematical operators in JavaScript are just as you'd expect: addition, subtraction, multiplication, division, and modulus (the remainder operator). Unlike the assignment operators, which combined assignment with math operations, these operators don't automatically add in the value on the left-hand side of an equation. Take a look at the following examples:

Operator	*Example*	*Meaning*
+	x = 1 + 3	x = 4 (addition)
-	x = 100 - 75	x = 25 (subtraction)
*	x = 6 * 7	x = 42 (multiplication)
/	x = 49 / 7	x = 7 (division)
%	x = 11 % 5	x = 1 (modulus)

Operator precedence

Just as in regular (non-Web-page-oriented) math, an order of evaluation is applied to a JavaScript statement that contains multiple operators. Unless you set phrases off with parentheses, the JavaScript interpreter observes the precedence order shown in the following table (from the parentheses, which has the highest order of precedence, to the comma, which has the lowest):

Operator	*Syntax*	*Explanation*
Parentheses	( )	For calling functions and grouping math expressions
Unary	--, ++, -, !	Decrement, increment, and negation operators
Mathematical	%, /, *, -, +	Modulus, division, multiplication, subtraction, addition
Relational	>=, >, <=, <	Greater than/equal to, greater than, less than/equal to, less than

Operator	Syntax	Explanation
Equality	! =, ==	Not equal to, equal to
Logical "and"	&&	If *all* expressions in a statement meet some criteria
Logical "or"	||	If *at least one* expression in a statement meets some criteria
Conditional	?:	(y < 0) ? x : y If y is less than 0 (whatever is before the ? is true), then return x (whatever is *before* the :), else return y (whatever is *after* the :)
Assignment	%=, /=, *=, -=, +=, =	Assignment + mathematical
Comma	,	Used for separating parameters in a function call

So, how exactly does this work? Well, suppose that the JavaScript interpreter runs into the following statement in your script:

```
alert("Grand total: " + getTotal() + (3 * 4 / 10) +
    tax++)
```

The JavaScript interpreter knows that its job is to evaluate the statement – so the first thing it does is scan the whole line. When the interpreter finds the first set of parentheses, it knows that's where it needs to start. It thinks to itself, "Okay, first I'll get the return value from `getTotal()`. Then I'll evaluate (3 * 4 / 10). Within (3 * 4 / 10), I'll do the division first, then the multiplication. Now I'll add one to the *tax* variable. Okay, the last thing I have to do is add the whole thing up to come up with a string to display."

If you don't want to go the trouble of memorizing the precedence order, that's okay. Just group expressions in parentheses. Because parentheses outrank all the other operators, you can effectively force JavaScript to override its default precedence order.

Special Operators

A couple of JavaScript operators, `typeof` and `void`, don't really fit into any other operator category. Take a look for yourself!

typeof

You can apply the `typeof` operator to any JavaScript object to find out what *type* the object is (when you know what type the object is, you then know what you can do to the object). For example, if you apply the `typeof` operator to a string, it returns "`string`"; if you apply the `typeof` operator to a number, it returns "number"; if you apply the typeof operator to true, it returns "boolean" — and so on, for every kind of object that exists. Here's a glimpse of typeof in action:

```
typeof "The Bell Jar"           // returns "string"
typeof true                     // returns "boolean"
typeof 69                       // returns "number"
typeof document.lastModified    // returns "string"
typeof Math                     // returns "function"
typeof someVariable             // returns variable
   type
```

void

The void operator is a strange beast — it's used to tell JavaScript to do *nothing*. Perhaps you think that there's not much call for an operator that does nothing. Well, you'd be right — *except* in one pretty important instance: when you want to create and use an object but bypass its requirements for some reason.

For example, suppose that you want to display an image in your Web page. Suppose that you also want to recognize when a user drags her mouse pointer across the image (so that you can display a different message in the status bar for each section of the image the mouse pointer passes over).

Well, you can create an image with the HTML <IMG> tag, but in order to recognize when a user's cursor passes over that image, you also need to define an additional object, called an *area*.

Now, the reason you need to define an area *and* an image is because you want to take advantage of the area's onMouseOver and onMouseOut event handlers, but you also want to take advantage of the image's surface area. How to get the best of both worlds? Define both and tie 'em together! The only catch is that when you define an area (which is nothing more than a big fat link), it expects you to define a URL to link *to*. Well, you don't *want* to link to anything. All you want to do is use the area's onMouseOver and onMouseOut events.

The solution? Give the area what it wants — a URL definition — but give it one that does *nothing*: in a word, give it void! Check out the following code to see exactly how that's done.

```
<MAP NAME="thistleMap">

<AREA NAME="topThistle" COORDS="0,0,228,318"
    HREF="javascript:void(0)"
onMouseOver="self.status='That mouse pointer sure
    feels nice'; return true"
onMouseOut="self.status='Thanks for visiting; come
    again!'; return true">
</MAP>
```

(continued)

(continued)

```
<IMG NAME="currentImage"
SRC="images/thistle.gif" ALIGN="MIDDLE"
   ALT="[Scottish thistles]" USEMAP="#thistleMap">
```

String operators

Most of JavaScript's operators are designed to work with numeric values. A few, though, are also useful for manipulating strings. In the following table, `stringA` has been assigned the value "moo" and `stringB` has been assigned the value "cow".

Operator	Syntax	Explanation
Addition (+)	`myString = stringA + stringB`	myString = "moocow"
Append (+=)	`myString = "hairy " += stringB`	myString = "hairy cow"
Equality (==)	`if (myString == "moocow")`	if myString is equal to "moocow"
Inequality (!=)	`if (myString != "moocow")`	if myString is not equal to "moocow"

Unary operators

Unary operators look a little strange to the uninitiated eye. They're very useful, though, so it's worth spending a minute or two to get familiar with them. In all these examples, x is initially set to 11.

Unary	Example (x = 11)	Result/Meaning	How Come?
!	`!(x == 5)`	true (negation)	11 isn't equal to 5
-	`x = -x`	x = -11 (negation)	Turns positive numbers negative and vice versa
++	`x = x++`	x = 11 (increment by 1)	++ *after* a var is applied *after* assignment
	`x = ++x`	x = 12	++ *before* a var is applied *before* assignment
--	`x = x--`	x = 11 (decrement by 1)	-- *after* a var is applied *after* assignment
	`x = --x`	x = 10	-- *before* a var is applied *before* assignment

Variables

A *variable* is a named placeholder for a value. You must do three things to a variable (if it is to be of any practical use): declare it, assign a value to it, and access it within its scope. The following sections show you how.

Accessing variables

After you declare a variable, you can then access it. By *accessing* a variable, I mean you can modify, display, or use the variable's value in a computation. Here's an example:

```
// Variable declaration and assignment
var myTitle = "Princess of the Universe"

// Displaying the value on the screen in a pop-up
    box
alert("Here is my title: " + myTitle)

//  Adding to the value
myTitle += " and everywhere else"

// Comparing one value to another
if (myTitle == "dog catcher") {
    alert("Memo to myself: At least I won the
    election!")
}
```

Assigning values to a variable

You can assign a value to a variable at the same time you declare it, or at any time after you declare it:

```
// Declaring and assigning all at once
var numberOfWineglasses = 6

// Assigning a value later in the program
numberOfWineglasses = 182

// Assigning a nonsensical value; OK by JavaScript
numberOfWineglasses = "cat food"
```

Declaring variables

Before you can use a variable, you have to declare it. You declare a variable in JavaScript by using the keyword `var`, as shown:

```
var myNumberVariable
var streetAddress
var anArrayOfJobTitles
```

JavaScript is what's known as a *loosely typed* language, which means that you don't have to tell the interpreter what kind of value you're going to assign to a variable right up front. All that you need is the `var` keyword and a unique variable name of your choice.

The name of your variable must begin with either a letter or an underscore. The variable name can contain numbers but no punctuation marks.

Understanding variable scope

A variable is only valid when it's *in scope,* which means that the variable has been declared between the same curly brace boundaries as the statement that's trying to access it.

For example, if you define a variable named `firstName` inside a function called `displayReport()`, you can only refer to it inside `displayReport()`'s curly braces. If you try to use the `firstName` variable from inside another function, you get an error. If you want to reuse a variable *among* functions (Eek! A global variable! Quick, call the cops!), you can declare it near the top of your script, before you declare any functions. That way, the variable's scope is the entire script, from the very first opening curly brace to the last — and all the functions defined within the script get to access it. Take a look at the following code example:

```
...
function displayReport() {
    var firstName = document.myForm.givenName.value
    ...
    alert("Click OK to see the report for " +
    firstName)
    // Using firstName here is fine; it was de-
    clared
    // inside the same set of curly braces as the
    // alert() method.
    ...
}
function displayGraph() {
    alert("Here's the graph for " + firstName) //
    Error!
    // firstName wasn't defined inside this
    // function's curly braces!
    ...
}
```

As you can see from the comments in the preceding code fragment, it's perfectly okay to use `firstName` inside the `displayReport()` function; `firstName` is in scope anywhere inside `displayReport()`. It's *not* okay, however, to use `firstName` inside `displayGraph()`. As far as `displayGraph()` is concerned, no such animal as `firstName` has been declared inside *its* scope!

Part III

HTML Objects: The Heart of It All

Because JavaScript is an object-based language, much of the JavaScript code you write involves HTML objects. Part II shows the relationship of each object in the JavaScript object hierarchy to one another, which provides a good overview of all the objects available to you. This part, though, is where you find all the details about the HTML objects used in JavaScript, the properties and methods that each object contains, and the event handlers that each object supports.

The sections in this part are cross-referenced so that you can look things up in different ways. For example, if you want to find out about a particular object, you can find it alphabetized in this part. On the other hand, if you know the name of a method but can't remember what objects are associated with it, check out Part VI, "Methods: How an Object Behaves." PartVI refers you to the objects each particular method supports.

In this part . . .

- ✔ Creating HTML objects (reprise)
- ✔ Invoking an object's methods
- ✔ Accessing an object's properties

About Objects

The two-bit definition of an *object* is "a software representation of some useful thing." JavaScript objects are no exception: Each of them are representations of the things that you need to build Web pages — push buttons, input fields, dates, and so on. Part I explains how to create each of the HTML objects in detail. This section focuses on the way these objects can be manipulated (that is, how their properties can be accessed and their methods invoked) with JavaScript statements.

For each element, you find three separate sections:

✦ How to create the object

✦ How to access the object's properties

✦ How to invoke the object's methods

For more detailed HTML syntax on how to create each object listed, *see also* Part I.

Remember that you create objects in HTML, but you work with objects in JavaScript. Therefore, you should place the code fragments in "Creating an object" between <HTML>...</HTML> tags. In contrast, you should place the code fragments in the "Accessing an object's properties" and the "Invoking an object's methods" sections between <SCRIPT>...</SCRIPT> tags.

anchor

An *anchor* is a piece of text that uniquely identifies a spot on a Web page. After you define an anchor — say, in the middle of a page — you (or anyone else for that matter) can set up a link so that when a user clicks the link, the page loads right where the anchor is located.

Creating an anchor:

```
<A NAME="TOC">Table of Contents</A>
```

Accessing anchor properties:

```
document.anchors.length
```

Invoking anchor methods:

The anchor object has no associated methods.

applet

The applet object corresponds to a Java applet embedded in an HTML form.

Creating an embedded applet:

```
<APPLET NAME="NervousApplet"
    CODE="NervousText.class" width=400 height=50>
<PARAM NAME="text" VALUE="Enter your text here.">
</APPLET>
```

Accessing applet properties:

The properties available to you depend on the specific Java applet with which you're working. One property should be available for *all* Java applets, however, and that's the name property:

```
document.applets[0].name
```

Invoking applet methods:

The applet methods available to you depend on the specific Java applet with which you're working. Ask the person who developed the Java applet that you're including in your Web page for a list of public methods that you can invoke on the applet.

area

The area object is used to make a specific area of an embedded image responsive to user events. You can make an area respond to a click event or to mouse pointer movement events.

Three separate HTML entities need to be defined as part of an area: an area (of course!), an HTML <MAP>, and an image. A complete example awaits you in the following code.

Creating an area:

```
<MAP NAME="thistleMap">

<AREA NAME="topThistle" COORDS="0,0,228,318"
    HREF="javascript:displayMessage()"
onMouseOver="self.status='When you see this mes-
    sage, click your left mouse button'; return
    true"
onMouseOut="self.status=''; return true">

</MAP>

<IMG NAME="currentImage"
SRC="images/thistle.gif" ALIGN="MIDDLE"
    ALT="[Scottish thistles]"
USEMAP="#thistleMap">
```

Instead of defining a URL value for the HREF attribute, the line looks like this:

```
HREF="javascript:displayMessage()"
```

This statement tells the JavaScript interpreter that it should invoke the custom function called displayMessage() when a user clicks on this area, *not* load a URL.

If you want to use the area event handlers onMouseOut and onMouseOver, but you don't want anything to happen when the user *clicks* on the area, assign the HREF attribute of <AREA> equal to this: "javascript:void(0)".

Accessing area properties:

No, this isn't a mistake — areas are stored in the links array.

```
document.links.length
document.links[0].hash
document.links[0].host
document.links[0].hostname
document.links[0].href
document.links[0].pathname
document.links[0].port
document.links[0].protocol
document.links[0].query
document.links[0].target
```

Invoking area methods:

No methods are associated with the area object.

button

A button object creates a push button on an HTML form.

Creating a button:

```
<FORM NAME="myForm">
<INPUT TYPE="button" NAME="inStateButton"
VALUE="In State" onClick="display(this)">
```

In this example, the name of the button is inStateButton, and the text displayed on the face of the button is "In State". When a user clicks on this button, the JavaScript interpreter calls the display() function and passes it one argument: the entire inStateButton object (denoted by this).

Accessing button properties:

```
document.myForm.inStateButton.name
document.myForm.inStateButton.type
document.myForm.inStateButton.value
```

The preceding JavaScript code fragments represent the button's name (inStateButton), type ("button"), and value ("In State"), respectively.

Invoking button methods:

```
document.myForm.inStateButton.click()
// used to click the button programmatically
```

checkbox

A checkbox object creates — well, a check box. A check box is like a toggle switch — its value is always either off or on.

Creating a check box:

```
<INPUT TYPE="checkbox" NAME="jazzCheckbox"
    VALUE="checkedJazz" CHECKED
    onClick="display(this)"> Click here if you like
    jazz.
```

In this example, the name of the check box is jazzCheckbox. The value is "checkedJazz" (which is the value that is submitted to the CGI program if the check box is checked). The checkbox is automatically checked the first time that it appears to the user; the text that appears next to the check box is "Click here if you like jazz."

Accessing check box properties:

```
document.myForm.jazzCheckbox.checked
document.myForm.jazzCheckbox.defaultChecked
document.myForm.jazzCheckbox.name
document.myForm.jazzCheckbox.type
document.myForm.jazzCheckbox.value
```

Invoking check box methods:

```
document.myForm.jazzCheckbox.click()
// used to set checkbox programmatically
```

document

A document object defines characteristics of the overall body of a Web page, such as the background color of a page, the default text color, and so on.

Creating a document:

```
<BODY BGCOLOR="lime" TEXT="maroon"
LINK="purple" ALINK="yellow" VLINK="blue"
    onLoad="welcome()"
onUnload="goodbye()"> </BODY>
```

The preceding code creates a Web page with a lime-colored background (yecch!) and maroon text. Link text appears purple at first, changes to yellow when a user clicks on the link, and then turns blue after the linked URL has been loaded. As you can see from the last two code statements, when the Web page is first loaded, the welcome() method is invoked automatically; when a user closes the Web page, the goodbye() method is invoked.

Accessing document properties:

```
document.alinkColor
document.anchors[0] // array of this document's
    anchors
document.bgColor
document.cookie
document.fgColor
document.forms[index] // array of this document's
    forms
document.lastModified
document.linkColor
document.links[index] // array of this document's
    links
document.location
document.referrer
document.title
document.vlinkColor
```

Invoking document methods:

```
document.clear()
document.close()
document.open("text/html")
document.write("Some text here")
document.writeln("Some more text here")
```

fileUpload

A fileUpload object consists of a Browse button and a text field. To specify a file name, users can either click on the Browse button and choose from the displayed list of files, or enter a filename directly into the text field.

Creating a fileUpload object:

```
<INPUT TYPE="file" NAME="myFileName">
```

Accessing fileUpload properties:

```
document.myForm.myFileUpload.name
document.myForm.myFileUpload.type
document.myForm.myFileUpload.value
```

Invoking fileUpload methods:

The fileUpload object has no associated methods.

In Netscape Navigator 3.0, the `fileUpload` object is read-only (you can't change its properties).

form

A *form* is used to gather input from users and to post data (including user input) to a server for additional processing.

Creating a form:

```
<FORM NAME="myForm" METHOD="POST" TARGET="_parent"
ACTION="http://altavista.digital.com/cgi-bin/
     query?pg=q&what=web&fmt=.&q=JavaScript"
ENCTYPE="multipart/form-data"
onSubmit="return verifyComplete()">
</FORM>
```

Accessing form properties:

```
document.myForm.action
document.myForm.elements[0].name
document.myForm.elements[0].value
document.myForm.encoding
document.myForm.length
document.myForm.method
document.myForm.target
document.forms[0]// first form defined in the
     document
document.forms.length //total # forms defined
```

Invoking form methods:

```
document.myForm.reset()
document.myForm.submit()
```

frame

A *frame* is a special kind of window. You can think of a frame as an individual pane of glass — that is, you can have several frames per regular window or just one. A user can scroll each frame independently.

Creating a frame:

```
<FRAMESET ROWS="50%,50%" COLS="40%,60%">
<FRAME SRC="framcon1.html" NAME="frame1">
<FRAME SRC="framcon2.html" NAME="frame2">
</FRAMESET>
```

Accessing frame properties:

```
frames.length
frames[0]name
```

(continued)

(continued)

```
frames[0].length
frames[0].parent
frames[0].self
frames[0].window
```

Invoking frame methods:

```
frames[0].blur()
frames[0].clearTimeout(timerID)
frames[0].focus()
timerID = frames[0].setTimeout("method(), 5000")
```

hidden

A *hidden* element is an input text field that doesn't appear on-screen.

Creating a hidden element:

```
<INPUT TYPE="hidden" NAME="markupPercent" VALUE=80>
```

Pretty straightforward, isn't it? The preceding line of code defines a hidden element named markupPercent and stuffs it with the initial value of 80 so that subsequent calculations can add an 80 percent markup to any purchase. (I think you can guess why a programmer might want to hide a value like this!)

Accessing hidden properties:

```
document.myForm.markupPercent.name
document.myForm.markupPercent.type
document.myForm.markupPercent.value
```

Invoking hidden methods:

The hidden object has no associated methods.

history

The history object contains a linked list of all the URLs that a user has visited from within a particular window. This object provides the list of URLs you see when you select the Go menu item in Navigator or Internet Explorer.

Creating a history object:

This one's a freebie; you don't have to write a lick of code to define the history object! The history object is defined for you by your Web browser. Each time you load a new Web page, your browser automatically adds that URL to the history object.

Accessing history properties:

```
history.length
```

Invoking history methods:

```
history.back()
history.forward()
history.go(-3)
```

image

The image object in JavaScript corresponds to the HTML <IMG> element. The image object represents an image embedded into a Web document.

At the time of this writing, Internet Explorer 3.0 does not support the image object.

JavaScript provides an Image constructor (the new keyword described in Part II) that you can use to create and load an image behind the scenes. You may want to load an image behind the scenes if you have a large image that you want to load while your user is doing something else. That way, when it's time to display the image, the image will already be loaded into memory so it will display right away. Here's how it works:

```
// To load the image, do this:
// first, create an image variable
var myImage = new Image()

// then, load the image into memory
myImage.src = "images/thistle.gif"

// Finally, to display the image, do this:
document.images[0].src = myImage.src
```

Creating an image:

```
<IMG NAME="currentImage"
SRC="images/jazzman.gif" ALIGN="MIDDLE" ALT="[Jazz
    guitarist]"
USEMAP="#jazzMap">
```

Accessing image properties:

```
document.myForm.currentImage.border
document.myForm.currentImage.complete
document.myForm.currentImage.height
document.myForm.currentImage.hspace
document.myForm.currentImage.lowsrc
document.myForm.currentImage.name
document.myForm.currentImage.prototypeName
document.myForm.currentImage.src
document.myForm.currentImage.vspace
document.myForm.currentImage.width
```

Invoking image methods:

No methods are associated with the image object.

link

A *link* is a piece of text (or an image) that loads another Web page when a user clicks on it. (A link often loads a specific spot, or *anchor,* on another Web page.)

Creating a link:

```
<A HREF="#TOC" onClick="verifyData()"
onMouseOver="displayScrollingText()" >Back to Table
    of Contents</A>
```

Accessing link properties:

```
document.links.length
document.links[0].hash
document.links[0].host
document.links[0].hostname
document.links[0].href
document.links[0].pathname
document.links[0].port
document.links[0].protocol
document.links[0].query
document.links[0].target
```

Invoking link methods:

Neither the link object nor the links array has any associated methods. (For more about arrays, **see also** Part IV).

location

Think of the location object as a mini-version of the history object. Instead of holding information on *all* the recently visited URLs, like the history object does, the location object contains information about just *one* URL — the one that's currently loaded.

Creating a location object:

Just like the history object, you don't have to write any code to define the location object — it's set up for you automatically by your Web browser.

Accessing location properties:

```
location.hash
location.host
location.hostname
location.href
location.pathname
location.port
location.protocol
location.search
location.target
```

Invoking location methods:

The location object has no associated methods.

Math

The Math object is the only built-in object in JavaScript. Unlike a built-in data type (such the ones shown in Part IV, which all describe a class of thing), the Math object not only describes a class of thing all right (a mathematical system) — but it also *implements* the class. Math contains properties and methods for all kinds of mathematical constants and functions, such as logarithms and square roots. Hey, why reinvent the wheel?

Creating a Math object:

You never define the Math object yourself; it's done for you automatically. All you have to do is reference it, as shown in the following examples.

Accessing Math properties:

```
Math.E
Math.LN2
Math.LN10
Math.LOG2E
Math.LOG10E
Math.PI
Math.SQR1_2
Math.SQRT2
```

Invoking Math methods:

```
Math.abs(23)
Math.acos(123)
Math.asin(1)
Math.atan(1)
Math.atan2(1)
Math.ceil(25.85)
Math.cos(0)
Math.exp(1)
Math.floor(25.85)
Math.log(1)
Math.max(5,15)
Math.min(5,15)
Math.pow(8,3)
Math.random()
Math.round(15.58)
Math.sin(0)
Math.sqrt(49)
Math.tan(0)
```

navigator

The `navigator` object contains information about the version of Navigator currently in use.

Creating a navigator object:

You never define the `navigator` object yourself; it's done for you automatically when you bring up your Web browser.

Accessing navigator properties:

```
navigator.appCodeName
navigator.appName
navigator.appVersion
navigator.complete

// The mimeTypes array elements must be accessed
// through the array, as shown
navigator.mimeTypes[0].description
navigator.mimeTypes[0].enabledPlugin
navigator.mimeTypes[0].suffixes
navigator.mimeTypes[0].type

// The plugins array elements must be accessed
// through the array, as shown
navigator.plugins[0].description
navigator.plugins[0].filename
navigator.plugins[0].length
navigator.plugins[0].name

navigator.userAgent
```

Invoking navigator methods:

```
navigator.javaEnabled()
```

password

A `password` object is a special text input field that displays asterisks on-screen in place of the characters that the user actually types, enabling users to type in sensitive information (like a password or financial information) without fear that someone peeking over their shoulder will get a glimpse.

Creating a password:

```
<INPUT TYPE="password" NAME="userPassword" SIZE=15
    VALUE="secret!">
```

Accessing password properties:

```
document.myForm.userPassword.defaultValue
document.myForm.userPassword.name
document.myForm.userPassword.type
document.myForm.userPassword.value
```

Invoking password methods:

```
document.myForm.userPassword.focus()
document.myForm.userPassword.blur()
document.myForm.userPassword.select()
```

plugin

Think of the plugin object as the space on an HTML form where the output of a plug-in appears. The plugin object has no associated properties or methods. To get information about plug-ins, you must access the navigator property called plugins.

Creating an embedded plugin:

```
<EMBED NAME="myEmbed" SRC="http://www.adobe.com/
    acrobat/3beta/PDFS/Times.pdf" WIDTH=450
    HEIGHT=450>
</EMBED>
```

Accessing plugin properties:

No properties are associated with the plugin object. Use the navigator.plugins array to access plugin properties.

Invoking plugin methods:

No methods are associated with the plugin object.

radio

A *radio* button is a toggle switch, something like a check box. Unlike a check box, though, radio buttons are often grouped in sets to allow users to select a *single* option from a list.

Creating a radio button:

```
What's your favorite time of day?
<INPUT TYPE="radio" NAME="timeChoice"
    VALUE="morningSelected" CHECKED
onClick="showValues(0)"> Morning
<INPUT TYPE="radio" NAME="timeChoice"
    VALUE="afternoonSelected"
onClick="showValues(1)"> Afternoon
<INPUT TYPE="radio" NAME="timeChoice"
    VALUE="eveningSelected"
onClick="showValues(2)"> Evening
```

Accessing radio properties:

```
document.myForm.timeChoice[index].checked
document.myForm.timeChoice[index].defaultChecked
document.myForm.timeChoice.length  // # of radio
    buttons
```

(continued)

(continued)
```
document.myForm.timeChoice[index].name
document.myForm.timeChoice[index].type
document.myForm.timeChoice[index].value
```

Invoking radio methods:

```
document.myForm.timeChoice[index].click()
```

reset

A `reset` object is a special kind of button. When a user clicks on a reset button, it clears out all the user-input values in a form and resets each field to its default value.

Creating a reset button:

```
<INPUT TYPE="reset" NAME="resetButton"
    VALUE="Reset"
onClick="reinitializeFormulas()">
```

Accessing reset properties:

```
document.myForm.resetButton.name
document.myForm.resetButton.type
document.myForm.resetButton.value
```

Invoking reset methods:

```
document.myForm.resetButton.click()
```

select

The `select` object is used to display both a single-selection list box and a scrolling multiple-selection list box.

Creating a select element:

```
<SELECT NAME="fave" SIZE=3 MULTIPLE
    onBlur="displayResult(this)">
<OPTION VALUE="popChosen" SELECTED> pop
<OPTION VALUE="rockChosen" > rock
<OPTION VALUE="dogsChosen" > dogs barking Jingle
    Bells
<OPTION VALUE="rapChosen" > rap
<OPTION VALUE="showChosen" > show tunes
<OPTION VALUE="africanChosen" > African classical
</SELECT>
```

Accessing select properties:

```
document.myForm.fave.length
document.myForm.fave.name
document.myForm.fave.options
document.myForm.fave.selectedIndex
document.myForm.fave.options[index].defaultSelected
```

```
document.myForm.fave.options[index].index
document.myForm.fave.options.length
document.myForm.fave.options[index].selected
document.myForm.fave.options[index].text
document.myForm.fave.options[index].type
document.myForm.fave.options[index].value
```

Invoking select methods:

```
document.myForm.fave.blur()
document.myForm.fave.focus()
```

Submit

A Submit object is a special kind of button that submits all of the user input values on a form to the server when a user clicks on the button.

Creating a Submit button:

```
<INPUT TYPE="submit" NAME="submitButton"
VALUE="Submit Form" onClick="verifyInput()">
```

Accessing submit properties:

```
document.myForm.submitButton.name
document.myForm.submitButton.type
document.myForm.submitButton.value
```

Invoking submit methods:

```
document.myForm.submitButton.click()
```

Clicking on the Submit button sends a form to the URL value specified in the form's HTML ACTION attribute. The data is sent as a series of attribute-value pairs, each pair separated by an ampersand (&).

text

The text object is a single-line input field. (If you want a multiple-line input field, see the textarea object, defined in the following section).

Creating a text element:

```
<INPUT TYPE="text" NAME="lastName" VALUE="your name
    here"
SIZE=30 onBlur="validate()" onChange="validate()">
```

Accessing text properties:

```
document.myForm.lastName.defaultValue
document.myForm.lastName.name
document.myForm.lastName.type
document.myForm.lastName.value
```

Invoking text methods:

```
document.myForm.lastName.focus()
document.myForm.lastName.blur()
document.myForm.lastName.select()
```

textarea

A `textarea` object is just like a `text` object, except that instead of defining one scrolling input line, the `textarea` object defines a multi-line scrolling text box.

Creating a textarea object:

```
<TEXTAREA NAME="directions" ROWS=4 COLS=60
onBlur="validate()" onChange="display()"
onFocus="welcome()" onSelect="changeMode()">
This is default text.  You can type right over it,
add to it, cut it, paste it, or copy it.
</TEXTAREA>
```

Accessing textarea properties:

```
document.myForm.directions.defaultValue
document.myForm.directions.name
document.myForm.directions.type
document.myForm.directions.value
```

Invoking textarea methods:

```
document.myForm.directions.focus()
document.myForm.directions.blur()
document.myForm.directions.select()
```

window

The `window` object is the top-level granddaddy object for all `document` objects, and you're given the first one gratis, compliments of the `<BODY>`...`</BODY>` tag pair. If you want to create *extra* windows, the following example is the way to do it.

If you do create multiple windows, remember to tack the new window's name (`myOtherWindow`, for example) in front of any associated property or method you access so that the interpreter knows which window you're referring to at all times.

Creating a window:

Here's the generic syntax for creating a window, followed by an example:

```
windowVar = open("URL", "windowName",
    ["windowFeatures"])

myOtherWindow = open("win2.html", "secondWindow",
    "toolbar=yes, location=yes, directories=yes,
    status=yes, menubar=yes, scrollbars=yes,
    resizable=yes, width=250, height=400")
```

Accessing window properties:

```
defaultStatus
frames
length
name
opener
parent
self
status
top
window
```

Invoking window methods:

```
alert("Form will be sent now...")
blur()
close()
confirm("Do you really want to quit?")
focus()
myOtherWindow = open("", "secondWindow",
    "toolbar=yes, location=yes, directories=yes,
    status=yes, menubar=yes, scrollbars=yes,
    resizable=yes, width=250, height=400")
prompt("Enter the file name:", "testfile.txt")
scroll(50, 100)
timeoutID=setTimeout("displayAlert()", 2500)
clearTimeout(timeoutID)
myOtherWindow.write("Here is myOtherWindow.")
```

Part IV

Data Types: Building Basic JavaScript Objects

Some kinds of objects, such as *dates* and *strings,* are really basic; they're so basic, in fact, that almost every script you'll ever write will probably contain a reference to them. Because they're so common, JavaScript thoughtfully provides built-in classes for them — but because JavaScript is loosely based on C, these classes are still referred to by the conventional name of *data types*.

Unlike the objects that you find in Part III, JavaScript data types don't have corresponding HTML tags — they're pure JavaScript constructs. You declare them inside the `<SCRIPT>...</SCRIPT>` tag pair by using JavaScript statements, as you can see in the following sections.

In this part . . .

✔ **Creating objects based on built-in data types**

✔ **Accessing object properties**

✔ **Invoking object methods**

Array

An Array is an indexed list of things called *elements*. Element values can be whatever you want them to be — numbers, strings, or even other objects. You can fill an array with elements when you create it by passing values to the array constructor, or you can create an empty array and fill it with elements later.

Arrays are useful whenever you want to keep track of a group of related items.

Syntax:

```
arrayName = new Array([element1, element2, ...
    elementN | arraySize])
```

Example:

```
var listOfPets = new Array("dog", "cat", "gerbil")
listOfPets[3]="bird"

// signals that 2 initial elements are expected,
    but
// the interpreter won't complain if you assign
    more
var favoriteFoods = new Array(2)
favoriteFoods[0]="frozen yogurt"
favoriteFoods[1]="barbecued beef"
favoriteFoods[2]="stir-fry" // 3 elements is okay

var toDoList = new Array()
```

Accessing array properties:

```
favoriteFoods.length
favoriteFoods.prototypeName
```

Invoking array methods:

```
favoriteFoods.join()
favoriteFoods.reverse()
favoriteFoods.sort()
```

The first two lines of the preceding example code create an array called listOfPets, which contains four entries: the first entry is "dog", the second, "cat", and so on. Here's a conceptual look at the listOfPets array:

[0] "dog"	// first element in the listOfPets array is "dog"
[1] "cat"	// second element in the listOfPets array is "cat"

[2]	"gerbil"	// third element in the listOfPets array is "gerbil"
[3]	"bird"	// fourth element in the listOfPets array is "bird"

Date

A Date object in JavaScript is just what it is in real life — a specific time including second, minute, hour, day, month, and year information. Any time you work with dates, you should use the Date object. You can create dates based on the current time or on values that you provide. You can modify and manipulate the date then to your heart's content.

Syntax:

```
dateName = new Date()
// if no parameters are passed to the constructor,
// the result is the current date/time

dateName = new Date("month day,
                year  hours:minutes:seconds")

dateName = new Date(year, month, day)

dateName = new Date(year, month, day, hours,
    minutes, seconds)
```

Example:

```
var today = new Date()
var birthday = new Date("October 21, 1973
    01:40:00")
var graduation = new Date(1990, 8, 6)
var wedding = new Date(92, 07, 12, 10, 30, 21)
```

Accessing Date properties:

You access the contents of a Date a little differently than you do the contents of other data types. Accessing Date properties (except one) is done by calling methods, as you can see in the following example.

One property, called prototype, is different from all the rest. You can use a prototype to create a new property for a Date object, and you can name the new property you create anything you want. For example, every instance of Date has built-in properties like hours, minutes, seconds, day, month, and year. Using prototype, you can add a brand-new property that's meaningful to you to all instances of Date. Check out the following example to see how to add a property called description to a date.

```
// create a new date variable called "today"
var today = new Date()

// create a new property for date objects called
// "description"
Date.prototype.description = null

// assign a value to the new date object property
today.description = "Today I lost my first tooth!"
```

In the preceding code, you first add the description property to the Date object and then add a value for the description property. For example, "Today I lost my first tooth!" is defined for the instance of Date called today.

Invoking Date methods

If you think about it, you can basically do only two things with a property after it's defined: You can *get* the value of the property to see what it is, and you can *set* the value of the property. Data types have predefined properties; you never have to define them yourself. All you have to worry about is getting values (which, for instances of Date, you do with what's affectionately known as *getter* methods, or *getters* for short) and setting values (using *setter* methods, or *setters*).

Date getters:

```
birthday.getDate()
birthday.getDay()
birthday.getHours()
birthday.getMinutes()
birthday.getMonth() // subtracts 1 from the correct
    value
birthday.getSeconds()
birthday.getTime()
birthday.getTimeZoneoffset() // undefined in
    Navigator 2.0
birthday.getYear()
birthday.toGMTString()
birthday.toLocaleString()
Date.UTC(1983, 6, 24, 2, 51, 8)
```

Date setters:

```
birthday.setTime(Date.parse("January 7, 1997"))
birthday.setDate(21)
birthday.setHours(3)
birthday.setMinutes(59)
birthday.setMonth(11)
birthday.setSeconds(50)
birthday.setTime(identicalTwinsBirthday.getTime())
birthday.setYear(82)
```

Function

In Part V, you see how you normally declare functions. In Navigator 3.0, you can use an alternative way to create a function — you can use the built-in Function object.

Syntax:

```
functionName = new Function([arg1, arg2, ... argN],
    functionBody)
```

Example:

```
var calcDogYears = new Function ("age", "return age
    * 7")
alert("If Spot is 4, he's " + calcDogYears(4) +
    " in people years")
```

The preceding example code defines a variable called calcDogYears, of type Function, which takes one parameter (age), and returns a value (specifically, whatever the value of age is, multiplied by seven). Then the function is called like this: calcDogYears(4)

When you declare a function, JavaScript compiles it once. On the other hand, when you create a function by using the Function object, the JavaScript interpreter has to evaluate the function each time it's called. You gain flexibility with the Function object because you can create new functions on the fly (perhaps based on some user input). However, you pay a price in reduced efficiency by using the Function object — your script may take longer to execute.

Accessing Function properties:

```
calcDogYears.arguments[0]
calcDogYears.arguments.length
calcDogYears.prototypeName
```

Invoking Function methods

The Function object has no associated methods.

Option

You can use an Option object to represent one of the options assigned to a single- or multiple-selection list box (a select element). You create the Option object first and then insert it into the associated select element's options array.

The Option constructor accepts four optional arguments, as shown in the following table:

Optional Arguments for the Option Constructor	
optionText	The text to display in the select list next to this option
optionValue	The value to be sent to the server when this option is selected
defaultSelected	Whether this option should be selected by default *(true* or *false)*
selected	Whether this option is currently selected *(true* or *false)*

Syntax:
```
optionName = new Option([optionText, optionValue,
    defaultSelected, selected])
selectName.options[index] = optionName
```

Example:
```
var blues = new Option("Blues music", "blues",
    true, true)
document.myForm.musicSelection[0] = blues
```

You can delete an Option from the options array of a select element like this:

```
document.myForm.musicSelection[0] = null
```

Deleting an element in an array causes the array to be compressed together, so if you delete the second element of an array containing three elements, the array then holds two elements — the first and the third.

Accessing Option properties:
```
blues.defaultSelected
blues.index
blues.prototypeName
blues.selected
blues.text
blues.value
```

Invoking Option methods

No methods are associated with the option object.

String

A String object is neither more nor less than a series of characters, usually surrounded by quotes, like this: "Ralph", "Henrietta and Bugsy", "123,456,789.00", or "1600 Pennsylvania Avenue". Using strings is the only way you can pass pieces of text around inside JavaScript. Unless you expect to do some arithmetic operations on a value, you probably want to work with the value in string form, which you can see exactly how to do in this section.

Syntax:

Two ways exist to create a string. One way is to use the built-in String data type; the other way is simply to surround the string value with double quotes ("like this"). Strings can be stored in variables but they don't have to be; when strings are not stored in variables, they're called *string literals*.

```
stringName = new String("some string") // one way
stringName = "some string" // another way
```

Example:

```
var lastName = "Smith" // a string variable
var firstName = new String("Barney") // a string
    variable
alert("Millions, including the "  // a string
    literal
        + lastName +
        "'s, enjoy JavaScript daily with their
    morning pastry.")
```

Accessing String properties:

```
lastName.length
String.prototype.description = null
middleName = new String("T.J.")
middleName.description = " T.J. doesn't actually
    stand for anything."
```

Invoking String methods:

```
lastName.anchor("tableOfContentsAnchor")
lastName.big()
lastName.blink()
lastName.bold()
lastName.charAt(3)
lastName.fixed()
lastName.fontcolor("springgreen")
lastName.fontsize(7)
lastName.indexOf("i")
```

(continued)

(continued)

```
"Ralph".italics()
"Ralph".lastIndexOf("r")
"Ralph".link("http://www.netscape.com")
"Ralph".small()
"Ralph".strike()
"Ralph".sub()
"Ralph".substring(0, 3)
"Ralph".sup()
"Ralph".toLowerCase()
"Ralph".toUpperCase()
```

Part V

Functions

A function is nothing more than a named group of JavaScript statements that, when called, execute all at once. Unlike methods, which are always associated with a particular object's data, functions don't belong to any particular object. Instead, functions adopt the values you pass to them (called *arguments*) when you invoke the function. ·

In this part . . .

✔ Understanding functions

✔ Creating your own custom functions

✔ Using functions to create instances of objects

✔ Calling built-in functions

About Using Functions

A *function* is nothing more than a named group of JavaScript statements. Every time you use, or *call,* the function, all the statements in the function are executed in one fell swoop. Although JavaScript provides a handful of built-in functions, you're not nearly as likely to use them as you are to use the custom functions that you define. You can find a complete list of all the built-in JavaScript functions, as well as steps for how to create your own functions later in this part. Whether they're built-in or custom-designed, though, you call all functions (with the exception of new) the very same way.

Calling a function

Remember, you must first define a function before you can call it.

Suppose you have access to a function called calculateTotal() (maybe you borrowed it, maybe you wrote it, maybe you purchased it). The purpose of this function is to calculate a total price based on the number of items a user wants to order and the price of each item.

Not surprisingly, this function takes two input parameters: one for the price, and the other to represent the number of items. calculateTotal() returns a number.

When you want to call a function, it's essential that you know three things:

✦ The correctly spelled name of the function

✦ The number and type of parameters the function expects

✦ What the function is supposed to return; for example, a number, a string, or whatever

The best way to find out the answer to these questions is to look at the function definition. If you created the file, the definition should be somewhere near the top of the HTML file. (Of course, if the function you're interested in calling is one of the built-in ones, it won't be defined in the HTML file — it's built right in! *See also* "Built-in Functions" later in this part for details on calling built-in functions.)

Since you know the name of the function (it's calculateTotal()), what it accepts (two numbers, one for the number of items and one for the price), and what it returns (a number), you can call the function, as shown in the following code:

```
var myPrice = calculateTotal(3, 19.95)
```

Defining a function

Creating, or *defining,* a function is easy as pie (whoever coined that phrase must have been better at rolling out pie crust than I am!). Here's the generic syntax for a function declaration:

```
function aName([parameter][, parameter]
    [..., parameter]){
    statements
}
```

Here's how the `calculateTotal()` function that was called in the preceding section may have been defined:

```
function calculateTotal(numberOrdered, itemPrice) {
    var result = numberOrdered * itemPrice
    return result
}
```

As you'd expect, this function multiplies the value for `numberOrdered` by the `itemPrice` and returns the result. *See also* "Creating a Custom JavaScript Function" later in this part.

Returning values

The `return` keyword is used to hand a value from a function back to whatever line of code called the function in the first place. The calling line of code can then use the returned value for anything it wants (to display it, use it in further calculations — that kind of thing). Technically, a function doesn't *have* to return a value but, in practice, most of them do. Here's the syntax for `return`:

```
return expression
```

You can see by the syntax that a function can return an expression, and an expression can be just about anything: a variable, a statement, or a complex expression. Check out these examples:

```
// returning a variable
return calculatedResult

// returning a statement
return (inputValue * 10

// returning a complex expression
return (someValue / 100 + ((anotherValue * 55) %
    9))
```

Make sure that the `return` statement is the very last statement in the body of your function. After all, `return` means just that — return. When the JavaScript interpreter hits the `return` statement, it returns to whatever line of code called it, right then and there, and continues interpreting the script. If you've placed statements inside the function after the `return` statement, they'll never be evaluated.

Built-in Functions

"Creating a Custom JavaScript Function," later in this part, describes how to create your very own functions. The handful of functions in this section, though, are freebies — they've already been created and are ready and waiting for you should you ever want to call them. Read on for real-life examples.

escape ( ) — encodes a string

Use the escape() function to encode special characters such as spaces, tabs, dollar signs, hash marks, exclamation points, and so on — so that the characters can be sent safely from one program (your Web page) to another program (a CGI program on a server). Then you can use unescape() on the other side, inside the CGI program, to decode the characters.

The string that returns from escape() is in the form "%xx", where *xx* is the ASCII encoding of each character in the argument. The *string* argument must be a nonalphanumeric string in the ISO Latin-1 character set (which, translated into English, means any character that's not an alphabetic character or a number). If you pass escape() a string containing numbers and punctuation marks by mistake, like this:

```
escape("67%@X")
```

escape() doesn't even attempt to encode the string — the function just returns the same string that you sent it.

Syntax:

```
escape(string)
```

Example:

```
encodedStringToPass = escape("& ")
// The above statement will return "%26%20"
```

eval ( ) — evaluates a string

The eval() function evaluates a string that contains a JavaScript phrase (as opposed to a regular old JavaScript phrase that's not inside a string) and returns the value. Sometimes the application of this function is really straightforward: Someone enters a number into a text field (for example, "82345") and you need to turn the value into an integer before you can use it in any numeric computations. (*See also* "isNaN( )" in the following section.) Other times, the application can be a bit more sophisticated, as shown in the following example.

Syntax:

```
eval(string)
```

Example:

```
var totalPrice = "((numberOrdered * price) * tax)"
if (noTaxRequired) {
    totalPrice = "(numberOrdered * price)"
}
...
// totalPrice prints out as a numeric value,
// not the string you see above
document.write(eval(totalPrice))
```

The preceding code snippet evaluates totalPrice (which has a string value) and displays the result on-screen.

isNaN ( ) — is not a number

The isNaN() function lets you determine whether a value is Not a Number. (Get it — isNaN?) This function returns *true,* or *1,* if the specified testValue is not a number. The function returns *false,* or *0,* if the testValue is a number. Your fifth-grade English teacher was right — double negatives are confusing! Unfortunately, many programming languages make liberal use of them.

Syntax:

```
isNaN(testValue)
```

Example:

```
if (isNaN(ageInputValue)) {
    alert("Please enter a number for the age
    field.")
}
```

parseFloat ( ) — turns strings into floating-point numbers

A *floating-point number* is any number that has a decimal in it (19.95, for example). Surprisingly, it's handy at times to be able to turn a string into a floating-point number. For example, what if you have the value "78.95" in one of your input fields and you want to use it in some calculations? As it stands, you can't; it's a string (you know it's a string because it's got quotes around it), and you can't do much in the way of mathematical calculations on strings. The solution is to convert the string value to a floating-point value by using the parseFloat() function and then perform your calculations.

If the string argument that you give parseFloat() can't be converted completely, the parseFloat() function behaves in one of two ways:

✦ If the very first character can't be converted, parseFloat() returns "NaN" (Not a Number).

✦ If the first character can be converted but a subsequent character can't, parseFloat() returns the floating-point value of everything it could convert, up until it encountered the invalid character.

Valid characters for the string argument include the numbers 0 through 9, plus (+), minus (–), decimal (.), and exponent (E).

Syntax:

parseFloat(*string*)

Example:

```
function isANumber(inputValue){
    answer=true
    for (var i=0; i<inputValue.length; i++) {
        if ((inputValue.charAt(i) != "0") &&
            !parseFloat(inputValue.charAt(i))) {
                answer=false
        break
        }
    }
return answer
}
```

The function in this example returns *false* if the argument sent to it is not a number, and *true* if it *is* a number. All the action is happening inside the if statement (which is itself buried inside a for loop). The if statement looks through the input value one character at a time and stops the minute that it encounters a character that can't be represented as a number.

parseInt () — *turns strings into integers*

Use the parseInt() function to turn specified *string* and *radix* arguments into an integer.

A *radix* isn't a strong-tasting root; it's a representation of a numbering system. The *radix* argument tells parseInt() which base you want the string converted to — for example, decimal (radix = 10), octal (radix = 8), hexadecimal (radix = 16), binary (radix = 2), and so on. Fortunately for the nongeeks among us, decimal is the default. If you don't specify a radix, the parseInt() function returns an integer in good old base 10, the very same numbering

system human beings use to communicate. (The parseInt()
function does convert strings to integers of different bases,
depending on what type of character is first in the string.)

If the string argument that you give parseInt() can't be converted completely, the function behaves in one of two ways:

✦ If the very first character can't be converted, parseInt()
returns "NaN" (Not a Number).

✦ If the first character can be converted but a subsequent
character can't, parseInt() returns the integer value of
everything that it could convert up until it encountered the
invalid character.

Valid characters for the string argument include the numbers 0
through 9 plus any other characters that are allowed by the radix
you choose.

Syntax:

```
parseInt(string [, radix])
```

Example:

```
parseInt("F", 16)        // base 16; returns 15
parseInt("17", 8)        // base 8; returns 15
parseInt("15", 10)       // base 10; returns 15
parseInt("15.99", 10)    // base 10; returns 15
parseInt("123")          // base 10; returns 123
parseInt("1111", 2)      // base 2; returns 15
```

unescape ( ) — decodes a string

As you can probably guess, unescape() is the opposite of
escape(). The escape() function encodes (or *escapes*) a string,
and unescape() decodes (or *unescapes*) a string. The *string*
argument can be in either of two forms:

✦ %*xx*, where *xx* is an integer between 0 and 255

✦ A hexadecimal number between 0x0 and 0xFF

The returned string will be a series of characters in the ISO Latin-1
character set (better known as the "non-numeric, non-punctua-
tion-mark character set").

Syntax:

```
unescape("string")
```

Example:

```
decodedString = unescape("%26%20") // returns "& "
```

Creating a Custom JavaScript Function

To create, or *declare,* a function in JavaScript, you need to use the `function` keyword as shown in the following example:

```
function functionName([parameter] [, parameter]
    [..., parameter]) {
    statements
    return returnExpression
}
```

As you can see in the preceding syntax, functions can accept parameters (also called *arguments*) — but they don't have to (the square brackets, as always, denote optional items). Here's the declaration for a function that accepts no parameters:

```
function displayCopyright() {
    alert("The content in this Web page is copy-
    righted by the XYZ Corporation."

    return true
}
```

And here's how you might call it:

```
<INPUT TYPE="button" NAME="displayCopyButton"
VALUE="View Copyright Info"
    onClick="displayCopyright()">
```

With a fixed number of parameters

Here's an example of a function named `computeTax()`, that requires two parameters: `price` and `taxRate`.

```
function computeTax(price, taxRate) {
    return (price * taxRate)
}
...
<INPUT TYPE="button" NAME="myButton" VALUE="Press
    me"
onClick='computeTax("19.95", .08)'>
```

With a variable number of parameters

You don't have to do anything special to declare a JavaScript function that accepts a variable number of parameters. All you need to do is send however many parameters you want to send to a regular function. Then, in the body of the function, you can capture all of the parameters and process them as you see fit. For example:

```
function myFunction(inputValue) {
    for (var i=0; i < myFunction.arguments.length;
```

```
        i++) {
            alert("Here's one: " +
                myFunction.arguments[i])
        }
    }
    ...
    <INPUT TYPE="button" NAME="myButton" VALUE="Press
        me"
    onClick='myFunction("arfie", "barfie", "snarfie")'>
```

You can see from its definition that myFunction() expects
just one parameter: inputValue. However, the function is being
called in the onClick event handler with *three* values – "arfie",
"barfie", and "snarfie". So, myFunction() quickly figures
out how many values were actually passed by examining the value
of myFunction.arguments.length. The function then proceeds
to display each of the three values to the user.

Functions that Help You Create and Work with Objects

When used in conjunction with a custom-built function that
defines a new type of object, the new operator enables you to
create an instance (or a dozen instances) of that type of object.
Here's how it works. First, take a look at a function that defines a
customer object. You can see from looking at this function that
every customer instance that you create will have an associated
name, age, sex, and occupation:

```
function customer(inputName, inputAge, inputSex,
                inputOccupation) {
    this.name = inputName
    this.age = inputAge
    this.sex = inputSex
    this.occupation = inputOccupation
}
```

Now that there's a "mold" available for creating customers, all you
need to do is use it. You can create as many customers (okay,
technically, instances of objects *representing* customers) as you like
by using the new keyword, as you can see in the following section.

new

(Technically, new isn't a function at all; it's an operator. It works
pretty much like a function, though, which is why it's presented in
this section.)

To create two separate objects representing customers, here's
what you do:

```
var firstCustomer = new customer("Junior Samples",
    56, "M", "car dealer")

var secondCustomer = new customer("Margaret
    Mannfred", 34, "F", "contractor")
```

this

You may have noticed the `this` keyword in the `customer` function declaration shown in the code for defining a `customer` object. Then again, maybe you didn't, so here it is again:

```
function customer(inputName, inputAge, inputSex,
            inputOccupation) {
    this.name = inputName
    this.age = inputAge
    this.sex = inputSex
    this.occupation = inputOccupation
}
```

In the preceding example, `this` is shorthand for the `customer()` function. When the JavaScript interpreter encounters the `this` keyword, the interpreter already knows it's inside a function called `customer()`; so it automatically substitutes `customer()` for the `this` keyword. That way you don't have to keep spelling out the whole function name yourself. (It also makes the code easier to read.)

with

`with` is a kind of shorthand that you can use to save yourself a few keystrokes. When you want to refer to several attributes of the same object (for instance, the attributes `lastModified`, `location`, and `title` of the `document` object), instead of writing this:

```
document.writeln(document.lastModified)
document.writeln(document.location)
document.writeln(document.title)
```

you can write this:

```
with (document) {
    writeln(lastmodified)
    writeln(location)
    writeln(title)
}
```

The JavaScript interpreter is satisfied with (and responds identically to) either version.

For more details about using functions in JavaScript, see *JavaScript For Dummies,* by yours truly, published by IDG Books Worldwide, Inc.

Part VI

Methods: How an Object Behaves

This part lists every method available to you in JavaScript.

In this part . . .

- ✓ Getting familiar with the methods available to you in JavaScript
- ✓ Deciding how (and when) to call each method

Methods

A *method* is just like a function (***see also*** Part V for more on functions). Unlike functions, however, methods access only one object's data — the object with which the method is associated. A method's name is typically a verb that describes what the method does to its associated object (for example, `blink()`, `blur()`, and `click()`). As you see in the upcoming examples, you invoke methods by specifying the fully qualified (that is, the *complete*) name of the object to which the method belongs.

Take the `click()` method, for example. If you have three buttons on a form — buttonOne, buttonTwo, and buttonThree, all of which support the `click()` method, how would the JavaScript inter-preter translate `click()` by itself? It couldn't! You have to include the method to specify *which* button you want to click on, like this: `document.myForm.buttonOne.click()`.

The only exception to this format is the `window` object, which doesn't usually need to be specified explicitly when you call one of its methods.

Several of the `String` methods that you run across in this part are identical to selected HTML tags in terms of their results. For example, two ways exist to make text on a Web page appear in big font, and each way is equally effective:

+ A JavaScript statement: `document.write("Here is some big text".big())`

+ An HTML statement: `<BIG>Here is some big text</BIG>`

Whenever you have a choice between using an HTML tag and a JavaScript statement to perform the same task, ask yourself whether you want to perform the task based on some user input. If so, opt for the JavaScript statement; if not, the HTML tag will suffice.

abs

Use the `abs()` method of the `Math` object to return the absolute value of a number.

Syntax:

`Math.abs(number)`

Example:

`var myResult = Math.abs(1)`

acos

Use the acos() method of the Math object to return the arc cosine (in radians) of a number.

Syntax:

```
Math.acos(number)
```

Example:

```
var myResult = Math.acos(1)
```

alert

Use the alert() method of the window object to display a pop-up dialog box that contains two elements: a message that you define and an OK button.

Syntax:

```
alert("message")
```

Example:

```
alert("Your order total is " + getOrderTotal())
```

anchor

Use the anchor() method of the String object to identify a string as an HTML anchor. After you define a string as an anchor, you can use the string as the target for a hypertext link. **See also** the "Link" section in Part III.

Syntax:

```
string.anchor(anchorName)
```

Example:

```
"Table Of Contents".anchor("TOC_anchor")
```

Using the anchor() method lets you define an anchor inside a JavaScript script; the <A>...</A> tag pair is the way to define an anchor in HTML. For example, you can replace the preceding example with the following HTML code:

```
<A NAME="TOC_anchor">Table of Contents</A>
```

Most programmers use HTML tags to define anchors unless they want to create a link on the fly, based on some user input. To define a link based on user input, savvy JavaScript authors use the anchor() method instead.

asin

Use the asin() method of the Math object to return the arc sine (in radians) of a number.

Syntax:

Math.asin(*number*)

Example:

Math.asin(1)

atan

Use the atan() method of the Math object to return the arc tangent (in radians) of a number.

Syntax:

Math.atan(*number*)

Example:

Math.atan(1)

atan2

Use the atan2() method of the Math object to return a numeric value for the angle (theta component) of the polar coordinate (r, theta) that corresponds to the specified Cartesian coordinate (x, y). (If you understood that sentence, congratulations! You're a rocket scientist.)

Syntax:

Math.atan2(*number*)

Example:

Math.atan2(90, 15)

back

Use the back() method of the history object to load the previous URL in the history list.

Syntax:

history.back()

Example:

history.back()

Invoking the back() method of the history object produces the
same result as history.go(-1). Choosing Go⇨Back from the
Navigator or Internet Explorer menu also produces the same
result, for that matter. If you know for sure that you only want to
go back one URL, the history.back() method is the way to go;
if you have to calculate how many URLs to go back, history.go()
is a better choice.

big

Using the big() method of the String object enables you to
display a string in big (size 4) font. (To specify font sizes from 1
through 7, *see also* "fontsize", described later in this part.)

Syntax:

string.big()

Example:

document.write("This is gonna be big!".big())

Using the big() method of the String object produces the same
result as surrounding text with the <BIG>...</BIG> HTML tag
pair. Typically, your choice of which method to use depends on
whether you know ahead of time what text you want to display in
big font. If you know what text should appear in big font, the HTML
tag works fine. On the other hand, if you need to display the text
dynamically, the string.big() method is your best bet.

blink

Using the blink() method of the String object enables you to
display a blinking string.

Syntax:

string.blink()

Example:

document.write("FREE".blink())

Using the blink() method of the String object produces the
same result as surrounding text with the <BLINK>...</BLINK>
HTML tag pair.

blur

Use the blur() method of the frame, password, select, text,
textarea, or window objects to remove focus from those objects.

(When you click on a form element and it lets you interact with the element, that element is said to have *focus;* when you click somewhere else, that element is said to *blur.*)

At the time of this writing, Internet Explorer 3.0 doesn't support `window.blur()`.

Syntax:

```
frameReference.blur()
passwordName.blur()
selectName.blur()
textName.blur()
textareaName.blur()
windowReference.blur()
```

Example:

```
parent.myFrame.blur()
document.myForm.myPassword.blur()
document.myForm.mySelectField.blur()
document.myForm.myTextField.blur()
document.myForm.myTextareaField.blur()
mySecondWindow.blur()
```

bold

Using the `bold()` method of the `String` object enables you to display a string in bold font.

Syntax:

```
string.bold()
```

Example:

```
document.write("IMPORTANT".bold())
```

Using the `bold()` method produces the same result as surrounding text with the `<B>...</B>` HTML tag pair.

ceil

For math geniuses, use the `ceil()` (for *ceiling*) method of the `Math` object to return the smallest integer that is greater than or equal to a specified number.

Syntax:

```
Math.ceil(number)
```

Example:

```
document.write("The ceil of 36.25 is " +
    Math.ceil(36.25))
```

charAt

Use the charAt( ) method of the String object to return one single character of a string given a specified index.

Syntax:

```
string.charAt(index)
```

Example:

```
// thirdLetter will get the value 't'
var thirdLetter = "Netscape".charAt(2)
```

clearTimeout

Use the clearTimeout( ) method of the frame or window objects to clear a timeout that was set by using the corresponding setTimeout( ) method. *See also* "setTimeout" later in this part for specifics.

Syntax:

```
clearTimeout(timeoutID)
```

Example:

```
readyYetTimer = setTimeout("alert('5 seconds has
    elapsed. Are you ready yet?!'), 5000"
...
clearTimeout(readyYetTimer)
```

click

Use the click( ) method of the button, checkbox, radio, reset, and Submit objects to simulate a mouse click programmatically (in other words, calling the click( ) method has the same effect as a user clicking on a button with the mouse). Clicking on a radio button selects the radio button (that is, sets the radio button's checked property to true). Clicking on a check box checks the check box (sets the check box's checked property to true).

Syntax:

```
buttonName.click( )
checkboxName.click( )
radioName[index].click( )
resetButtonName.click( )
submitButtonName.click( )
```

Example:

```
document.myForm.myButton.click( )
document.myForm.myCheckbox.click( )
```

(continued)

(continued)
```
document.myForm.myRadioGroup[0].click()
document.myForm.myReset.click()
document.myForm.mySubmit.click()
```

close (document)

Use the `close()` method of the `document` object to close an
output stream that was opened with the `document.open()`
method and to force any data already sent to the document to be
displayed. *See also* the "open (document)" and "open (window)"
sections later in this part.

Syntax:

```
document.close()
```

Example:

```
myMessageWindow=window.open('', 'messageWindow')
myMessageWindow.document.writeln('This is a message
    window, all right!')
myMessageWindow.document.close()
```

close (window)

Use the `close()` method of the `window` object to close a window
that was opened with the `open()` method of the `window` object.

As you'd expect, if you leave off a specific reference to a window,
the interpreter assumes that you want to close the current
window — with one exception. In an event handler, you must
specify `window.close()` if you want to close the current window.
(If you leave off the specific reference to a window, the current
document closes. Go figure.)

Syntax:

```
windowReference.close()
```

Example:

```
close() // closes the current window
```

```
// closes the current window from inside an event
    handler
window.close
```

```
// closes the window called myMessageWindow
myMessageWindow.close()
```

confirm

Use the `confirm()` method of the `window` object to display a
pop-up dialog box on a Web page. The dialog box that appears

contains a message, an OK button, and a Cancel button. The
confirm() method returns *true* if the user clicks on the OK
button and *false* if the user clicks on the Cancel button.

Syntax:

```
confirm("message")
```

Example:

```
var submitOk = confirm("Do you really want to
    submit the form?")
```

The preceding code example causes a confirmation box to pop
up and ask the user, "Do you really want to submit the form?" If
the user clicks on the OK button, submitOk is set to true; but if
the user clicks on the Cancel button, submitOk is set to false.

cos

Use the cos() method of the Math object to return the cosine of a
number.

Syntax:

```
Math.cos(number)
```

Example:

```
Math.cos(0)
```

exp

Use the exp() method of the Math object to return e^{number}, where e
is Euler's constant and *number* is the number argument provided
to exp().

Syntax:

```
Math.exp(number)
```

Example:

```
Math.exp(1)
```

fixed

Using the fixed() method of the String object enables you to
display a string in fixed-pitch font. (Fixed-pitch font looks sort of
like the font from an old typewriter.)

Syntax:

```
string.fixed()
```

Example:

```
document.write("E = MC2".fixed())
```

Using the `fixed()` method produces the same result as surrounding text with the `<TT>...</TT>` HTML tag pair.

floor

Use the `floor()` method of the `Math` object to return the biggest integer that is less than or equal to a specified number.

Syntax:

```
Math.floor(number)
```

Example:

```
var result = Math.floor(88.78)
```

focus

Use the `focus()` method of the `frame`, `password`, `select`, `text`, `textarea`, or `window` objects to give them focus.

The `focus()` method is handy for helping users navigate through your form. For example, if you attempt to validate an input value and determine that the value is incorrect, you can set focus back to the input field so that the user can retype the value without first having to tab backward to it.

At the time of this writing, Internet Explorer 3.0 doesn't support `window.focus()`.

Syntax:

```
frameReference.focus()
passwordName.focus()
selectName.focus()
textName.focus()
textareaName.focus()
windowReference.focus()
```

Example:

```
self.frame1.focus()
document.myForm.myPassword.focus()
document.myForm.mySelectField.focus()
document.myForm.myTextField.focus()
document.myForm.myTextareaField.focus()
mySecondWindow.focus()
```

fontcolor

Using the fontcolor() method of the String object enables you to display a string in any conceivable color. *See also* Appendix B for a complete list of predefined colors; *see also* "Adding Multimedia to Your Web Page" in Part IX for instructions on creating your own colors.

Syntax:

```
string.fontcolor(color)
```

Example:

```
// using a predefined color string
document.write("This is brown".fontcolor("brown"))

// using hexadecimal RGB triplet notation
document.write("This is
    fuchsia".fontcolor("FF00FF"))
```

Using the fontcolor() method produces the same result as surrounding text with the <FONT COLOR="brown">...</FONT> HTML tag pair. Both the fontcolor method and the <FONT>...</FONT> tag pair override the default text color defined with the TEXT attribute of the <BODY>...</BODY> tag pair.

fontsize

Using the fontsize() method of the String object enables you to display a string in one of seven font sizes (where *size* must be an integer between 1 and 7).

Syntax:

```
string.fontsize(size)
```

Example:

```
var smallSize=1
document.write("This is large".fontsize(7))
document.write("This is small".fontsize(smallSize))
```

Using the fontsize() method produces the same result as surrounding text with the <FONTSIZE=7>...</FONTSIZE> HTML tag pair.

forward

Use the forward() method of the history object to load the next URL in the history list.

Syntax:

```
history.forward()
```

Example:

```
history.forward() // What could be easier?
```

Invoking the forward() method produces the same result as using history.go(1) (or choosing Go⇨Forward from the Navigator or Internet Explorer menu).

getDate

Use the getDate() method of a Date object to access the day of the month associated with a specified date. For example, if the Date object represents the 26th of June, 1996, getDate() returns the value *26*.

Syntax:

```
dateObjectName.getDate()
```

Example:

```
var today = new Date() // gets the current date
var dayOfMonth = today.getDate()
```

getDay

Use the getDay() method of a Date object to access the day of the week associated with a specified date (Monday being 1; Tuesday being 2; and so on, with Sunday being 7). For example, if the Date object represents Wednesday, the 26th of June, 1996, getDay() returns the value *3*.

Syntax:

```
dateObjectName.getDay()
```

Example:

```
var today = new Date() // gets the current date
var dayOfWeek = today.getDay()
```

getHours

Use the getHours() method of a Date object to access the hour (in 24-hour military time) associated with a specified date. For example, if the Date object represents Wednesday, the 26th of June, 1996, at 3:45 p.m., getHours() returns the value *15*.

Syntax:

```
dateObjectName.getHours()
```

Example:

```
var today = new Date() // gets today's date
var hour = today.getHours()
```

getMinutes

Use the getMinutes() method of a Date object to access the minutes associated with a specified date. For example, if the Date object represents Wednesday, the 26th of June, 1996, at 3:45 p.m., getMinutes() returns the value *45*.

Syntax:

dateObjectName.getMinutes()

Example:

```
var today = new Date() // gets today's date
var numberMinutesAfterTheHour = today.getMinutes()
```

getMonth

Use the getMonth() method of a Date object to access the month of the year associated with a specified date. For example, if the Date object represents Wednesday, the 26th of June, 1996, at 3:45 p.m., getMonth() returns the value *5*.

For a date of June, you'd think getMonth() would return *6*, wouldn't you? Well, unfortunately, it returns *5*. That's because JavaScript counts January as month 0, February as month 1, and so on.

Syntax:

dateObjectName.getMonth()

Example:

```
var today = new Date() // gets today's date
var month = today.getMonth()
```

getSeconds

Use the getSeconds() method of a Date object to access the number of seconds in the specified date. For example, if the Date object represents Wednesday, the 26th of June, 1996, at 3:45:16 p.m., getSeconds() returns the value *16*.

Syntax:

dateObjectName.getSeconds()

Example:

```
var today = new Date() // gets the current date
var seconds = today.getSeconds()
```

getTime

Use the `getTime()` method of a `Date` object to access the number of milliseconds that have elapsed since January 1, 1970, at 00:00:00 (no, I'm not kidding!). About the only use that regular folks are going to have for this method is to assign one time to another, like this: `timeToLeave = today.getTime()` (That way you never have to actually look at and decipher the darn thing.)

Versions of Navigator earlier than 3.0 (and some early beta versions of Internet Explorer Version 3.0) tend to — well — blow up if they encounter a date earlier than January 1, 1970. So avoid giving these browsers a date like this! If you're running anything other than Navigator 3.0 and want to work with dates older than 1970, try using a more recent date (say, 1980) and then doing subtraction by using regular variables (as opposed to `Date` objects). *See also* the "Date" section in Part IV.

Syntax:

```
dateObjectName.getTime()
```

Example:

```
var startDay = new Date() // gets the current date
var startTime = today.getTime()
```

getTimezoneOffset

Use the `getTimezoneOffset()` method of the `Date` object to get the difference in minutes between the time of the `Date` object and Greenwich Mean Time (GMT).

Syntax:

```
dateObjectName.getTimezoneOffset()
```

Example:

```
today = new Date() // gets the current date
currentTimezoneOffsetInHours =
    today.getTimezoneOffset()/60
```

getYear

Use the `getYear()` method of a `Date` object to access the year of the specified date (less 1900). For example, if the `Date` object represents Wednesday, the 26th of June, 1996, at 3:45:16 p.m., `getYear()` returns the value *96*.

Syntax:

```
dateObjectName.getYear()
```

Example:

```
var today = new Date() // gets the current date
var currentYear = today.getYear()
```

go

Use the go() method of the history object to load a URL from the history list. You can supply go() with one of the following two parameters:

+ An integer, which the interpreter uses to count forward (positive integer) or backward (negative integer) from the current list position to find a URL to load

+ A string that contains a whole URL or just part of a URL; the interpreter finds the nearest matching URL and loads it

Syntax:

```
history.go(delta | "location")
```

Example:

```
history.go(3) // loads the third URL forward
history.go(-2) // loads the second URL back

// loads the closest URL containing the parameter
    string
history.go("www.austin")
```

indexOf

Use the indexOf() method of the String object to search a specified string for the occurrence of another specified string. The indexOf() method accepts two parameters:

+ A search value that consists of a string for which to search

+ An optional index value that tells the interpreter where in the original string to begin searching for the search string (the default value is 0, which means that the search begins — where else? — at the beginning)

indexOf() returns the first index of the original string that matches the search string (see the following real-life example). If it can't find a match at all, it returns *-1*.

Syntax:

```
string.indexOf(searchValue, [fromIndex])
```

Example:

```
var theResult = "Can you can-can?".indexOf("can")
// theResult is set to 8
```

C a n   y o u   c a n -

0 1 2 3 4 5 6 7 **8** 9 10 11

The string "Can you can-can?" is nothing more than an indexed list of characters. As shown in this example, the first occurrence of "can" starts at index 8 — so theResult is set equal to 8.

italics

Using the italics() method of the String object enables you to display an italicized string.

Syntax:

```
string.italics()
```

Example:

```
"IMPORTANT".italics()
```

Using the italics() method produces the same result as surrounding text with the <I>...</I> HTML tag pair.

javaEnabled ( )

The javaEnabled() method of the navigator object returns *true* or *false,* depending on whether Java is enabled or disabled.

Syntax:

```
navigator.javaEnabled()
```

Example:

```
if (navigator.javaEnabled()) {
    alert("Java is enabled in this Navigator ses-
    sion.")
}
```

At the time of this writing, only Navigator 3.0 supports the javaEnabled() method.

join

The join() method of the array object joins the elements of an array into one long string. join() accepts an optional separator argument. If an optional separator argument is provided, it's placed between the elements inside the string. If no separator is provided, a comma is used to join the elements.

Syntax:

```
string = arrayName.join([separator])
```

Example:

```
var animalArray = new Array("cat", "dog", "bat",
    "bear")
var aString = animalArray.join(" and ")
// aString is assigned "cat and dog and bat and
    bear"
```

lastIndexOf

The lastIndexOf() method is practically a mirror image of the indexOf() method. lastIndexOf() starts searching from the *end* of the original string; indexOf() starts searching from the *beginning* of the original string.

Use the lastIndexOf() method of the String object to search a specified string backwards for the occurrence of another specified string. The lastIndexOf() method accepts two parameters:

✦ A search value that consists of a string for which to search

✦ An optional index value that tells the interpreter where in the original string to begin searching for the search string (the default value is length of the string minus one, which means that the interpreter begins searching at the end of the string)

The lastIndexOf() method returns the last index of the original string that matches the search string. If it can't find a match at all, it returns *–1*.

Syntax:

```
string.lastIndexOf(searchValue, [fromIndex])
```

Example:

```
var theResult = "Can you can-can?".lastIndexOf
    ("can")
// theResult is set to 12
```

link

Use the link() method of the String object to create an HTML hypertext link inside a JavaScript script. Remember to use the write() or writeln() methods of the document object to display the link. (It doesn't do much good to define a link on-the-fly if no one can see it to click on it, now does it?)

Syntax:

```
linkText.link(hrefAttribute)
```

Example:

```
document.write("My Cool Web Page".link("http://
    www.fictitious.com/me/my.html"))
```

log

Use the `log()` method of the `Math` object to return the natural logarithm (base *e*) of a number.

Syntax:

```
Math.log(number)
```

Example:

```
Math.log(10)
```

max

Use the `max()` method of the `Math` object to return the greater of two numbers.

Syntax:

```
Math.max(number1, number2)
```

Example:

```
var taxedAmount = Math.max(amount.calcOneWay(),
    amount.calcAnotherWay()) // pay taxes on
    greatest amount
```

min

Use the `min()` method of the `Math` object to return the lesser of two numbers.

Syntax:

```
Math.min(number1, number2)
```

Example:

```
var youngest = Math.min(myAge, georgesAge)
```

open (document)

Use the `open()` method of the `document` object to open a document for writing via the `write()` and `writeln()` methods. (Well, technically you're opening something called an output *stream,* but you can think of the stream as the document.) When you use the open() method, be sure to use the corresponding close() method as well. *See also* the "close (document)" section earlier in this part.

The open() method accepts one optional parameter, mimeType. mimeType (which refers to MIME type, or *Multipurpose Internet Mail Extension*) is a string that specifies the format of the data that you plan to stick into the document. Most of the time, you don't have to specify a value for this parameter; it defaults to plain old HTML, which is probably what you want. Just in case, though, the following table shows your choices:

MIME type	What It Is
text/html	HTML statements (this is the default)
text/plain	Plain old ASCII text with end-of-line characters
image/gif	An image in .GIF format
image/jpeg	An image in .JPG format
image/x-bitmap	An image in bitmap format
plugIn	A Netscape plug-in

Syntax:

```
document.open(["mimeType"])
```

Example:

```
document.open()
document.open("image/gif")
```

open (window)

Use the open() method of the window object to open a new Web browser window.

Syntax:

```
[windowVar = ] [window].open("URL", "windowName" [,
    "windowFeatures"])
```

Example:

```
secondWindow = open("", "statusWindow",
    "scrollbars=yes,width=200,height=200")
```

For the last optional value shown in the syntax sample (windowFeatures), you have your choice of any or all of following features. Just make sure that you surround the entire list that you create with quotes and separate each attribute-value pair with a comma (no spaces), as shown in the example. (The items bounded by square brackets are optional, and the pipe symbol means *or*.)

```
toolbar[=yes|no]|[=1|0],
location[=yes|no]|[=1|0],
directories[=yes|no]|[=1|0],
status[=yes|no]|[=1|0],
menubar[=yes|no]|[=1|0],
scrollbars[=yes|no]|[=1|0],
resizable[=yes|no]|[=1|0],
width=pixels,
height=pixels
```

parse

Use the parse() method of a Date object to turn a string into a date.

Syntax:

```
Date.parse(dateString)
```

Example:

```
myBirthday.setTime(Date.parse("Jul 26, 1996"))
```

pow

Use the pow() method of the Math object to return a specified base to the specified exponent power.

Syntax:

```
Math.pow(base, exponent)
```

Example:

```
document.write("7 to the power of 8 is " +
    Math.pow(7,8))
```

prompt

Use the prompt() method of the window object to display a pop-up dialog box that contains a message that you define, an input field, an OK button, and a Cancel button. The optional parameter inputDefault pre-fills the input field with the default value that you specify.

Syntax:

```
prompt("message" [, inputDefault])
```

Example:

```
prompt("What size t-shirt do you want?", "Large")
```

random

Use the random() method of the Math object to return a random number between 0 and 1.

Syntax:

```
Math.random()
```

Example:

```
var aRandomNumber = Math.random()
```

reload

The reload() method of the location object forces a reload of the document specified by the URL in the href property of the location object. The result of the reload() method is the same as clicking on the Reload button in Navigator (or the Refresh button in Internet Explorer).

Syntax:

```
windowReference.location.reload()
```

Example:

```
<INPUT TYPE="button" NAME="reloadButton"
VALUE="Reload Now"
onClick="self.location.reload()">
```

At the time of this writing, only Navigator 3.0 supports the reload() method.

replace

The replace() method of the location object replaces the current history entry with the specified URL.

The upshot is that after JavaScript calls the replace() method, the new URL loads, and the user can no longer navigate to the previously loaded URL by clicking on the Back button.

Syntax:

```
windowReference.location.replace("URL")
```

Example:

```
self.location.replace("http://home.netscape.com")
```

At the time of this writing, only Navigator 3.0 supports the replace() method.

reset

The reset() method of the form object simulates a user clicking on a Reset button; that is, it causes all a form's elements to be reset to their default values.

Using the reset() method can make entering multiple copies of your form easier for users. When users finish filling out your form and submit it, you can call the reset() method to reset the form so they can fill it out again from scratch.

Syntax:

```
document.formName.reset()
```

Example:

```
if (resetOkay) {
    document.myForm.reset()
}
```

At the time of this writing, only Navigator 3.0 supports the reset() method.

reverse

The reverse() method of the array object transposes the elements of an array; that is, the order of the elements is reversed (the first element becomes the last and the last element becomes the first).

Syntax:

```
arrayName.reverse()
```

Example:

```
var listOfJobs = new Array("bookie", "writer",
    "nurse")
listOfJobs.reverse()
// Now the array is in this order:  nurse, writer,
    bookie
```

round

The round() method of the Math object returns the value of a specified number, rounded to the nearest integer.

Syntax:

```
Math.round(number)
```

Example:

```
var closeEnough = Math.round(totalPrice)
```

scroll

The scroll() method of the window object lets you scroll a window to the coordinates you specify. scroll() accepts two arguments: an x-coordinate and a y-coordinate. Both values must be integers representing the number of pixels to scroll in each direction (the x-coordinate is left-to-right, and the y-coordinate is up-and-down).

This method only executes if the page the method is on contains enough displayed data to be scrollable. Put another way, unless the page is so long that scroll bars are seen, calling scroll() won't have a visible effect.

Syntax:

```
windowReference.scroll(x-coordinate, y-coordinate)
```

Example:

```
if(okayToScroll) {
    self.scroll(50, 100)
}
```

At the time of this writing, only Navigator 3.0 supports the scroll() method.

select

Use the select() method of the password, text, or textarea objects to select (highlight) their respective input areas.

Syntax:

```
passwordName.select()
textName.select()
textareaName.select()
```

Example:

```
onBlur="document.myForm.myPasssword.select()"
onClick="document.myForm.myTextField.select()"
if (goBack()) {
    document.myForm.myTextareaField.select()
}
```

setDate

Use the setDate() method of the Date object to set the day of the month for a specified date. The required dayValue parameter can be any integer from 1 to 31.

Syntax:

```
dateObjectName.setDate(dayValue)
```

Example:

myBirthday.setDate(26)

setHours

The setHours() method of the Date object enables you to set the hours for a specified date. The required hoursValue parameter can be any integer between 0 and 24. (For any value over 24, the interpreter adds the excess onto the days portion of the date.)

Syntax:

dateObjectName.setHours(hoursValue)

Example:

contractDate.setHours(12)

setMinutes

The setMinutes() method of the Date object enables you to set the minutes for a specified date. The required minutesValue parameter can be any integer between 0 and 60. (For any value over 60, the interpreter adds the excess onto the hours portion of the date.)

Syntax:

dateObjectName.setMinutes(minutesValue)

Example:

averageHeeHawEpisode.setMinutes(30)

setMonth

The setMonth() method of the Date object enables you to set the month for a specified date. The required monthValue parameter can be any integer between 0 and 11, where 0 corresponds to January and 11 corresponds to December. (For any value over 11, the interpreter adds the excess onto the years portion of the date.)

Syntax:

dateObjectName.setMonth(monthValue)

Example:

christmas.setMonth(11)

setSeconds

The setSeconds() method of the Date object enables you to set the seconds for a specified date. The required secondsValue parameter can be any integer between 0 and 59. (For any value over 59, the interpreter adds the excess onto the minutes portion of the date.)

Syntax:

dateObjectName.setSeconds(secondsValue)

Example:

pickyDate.setSeconds(12)

setTime

The setTime() method of the Date object enables you to set the date and time for a specified date. The required timeValue parameter reflects the number of milliseconds since January 1, 1970 00:00:00. (The fact that no normal human could come up with such a parameter should give you a tip-off that this method is mainly used to assign one date to another, like this: oneDate.setTime(anotherDate.getTime().)

Syntax:

dateObjectName.setTime(timeValue)

Example:

husbandAnniversary.setTime(wifeAnniversary.getTime())

setTimeout

Use the setTimeout() method of the frame or window objects to evaluate an expression after a specified length of time elapses. Using the setTimeout() method is just like setting a timer and then doing something when the timer goes off. (An obvious application for this method is a Web game: You can start the clock ticking when a user begins the game and then pop up a message saying Game Over if the user hasn't completed the game in a certain amount of time.)

This method takes the following two parameters:

✦ An expression to evaluate

✦ A number that represents the number of milliseconds to wait before evaluating the expression

Saving the return value from the setTimeout() method in a variable is a really good idea because you need to use this variable if you ever want to cancel the timer. To cancel a timer, you need to pass the variable you saved to the clearTimeout() method of the frame or window object (see the example of clearTimeout() in the following example for clarification).

Syntax:

```
timeoutID=setTimeout(expression, number)
```

Example:

```
readyYetTimer=setTimeout("alert('5 seconds has
    elapsed. Are you ready yet?!'), 5000"
...
clearTimeout(readyYetTimer)
```

setYear

The setYear() method of the Date object enables you set the year for a specified date. The required yearValue parameter must reflect a year between 1970 and 1999. (And because the range is so narrow, you don't have to specify the 20th century; for example, 1985 and 85 are both perfectly acceptable entries.)

Passing a *bogus* (out-of-range) value for the yearValue parameter shown in the following example may not cause an immediately obvious error. Because the interpreter assumes that every date falls in the 1900s, any value not between 70 (1970) and 99 (1999) has the effect of setting the date to the last day of 1969. No fireworks, no pop-up warnings — just really goofy date calculations.

Syntax:

```
dateObjectName.setYear(yearValue)
```

Example:

```
nephewGraduation.setYear(98)
```

sin

Use the sin() method of the Math object to return the sine of a number (*not* the number of sins committed!).

Syntax:

```
Math.sin(number)
```

Example:

```
document.write("Here is the sine of PI: " +
    Math.sin(Math.PI))
```

small

Using the small() method of the String object enables you display a string in small font ("small" equates to font size 2). *See also* the fontsize() method described earlier in this part.

Syntax:

string.small()

Example:

"This is gonna be really teensy.".small()

Using the small() method of the String object produces the same result as surrounding text with the <SMALL>...</SMALL> HTML tag pair.

sort

Use the sort() method of the array object to sort the elements in an array. The sort() method accepts an optional argument that specifies a function name to use for the sorting algorithm. If a function name isn't supplied, sort() converts the elements in the array to strings (if they're not already strings) and compares them in *lexicographic*, or alphabetic, order.

The default sorting algorithm may be sufficient for your needs — unless your array elements contain numbers. But look what happens if your array *does* contain numeric values: 60, 9, and 100 will be sorted like this — "100", "60", "9" — which is probably not what you expected. The following example contains code for a numeric sorting algorithm that, when passed to the sort() method, causes numbers to sort correctly.

Syntax:

arrayName.sort([*compareFunction*])

Example:

```
// this sort works just fine for string elements
anArray.sort()

// This function returns the lesser of two values.
// JavaScript automatically calls this function
// as many times as necessary, comparing two
// values at a time, until the entire array
// of elements is sorted.
function compareNumbers(a, b) {
    return a - b
}
...
anArrayOfNumbers.sort(compareNumbers)
```

split

Use the split() method of the String object to split a string
into an array of smaller strings. split() accepts an optional
separator which, if provided, is used to determine where the string
is divided. If no separator is provided, the resulting array consists
of one element containing the entire original string.

Syntax:

```
string.split([separator])
```

Example:

```
arrayOfWords = "There once was a man from
    Nantucket".split(" ")
```

Internet Explorer 3.0 does not support the split() method at the
time of this writing.

sqrt

Use the sqrt() method of the Math object to return the square
root of a number. If the number parameter is negative, the return
value is always 0. (Some math rule or something.)

Syntax:

```
Math.sqrt(number)
```

Example:

```
document.write(The square root of 36 is " +
    Math.sqrt(36))
```

strike

Using the strike() method of the String object enables you to
display a string with strikeovers so the text looks like it's been
crossed out.

Syntax:

```
string.strike()
```

Example:

```
"Was $49.99".strike()
```

Using the strike() method produces the same result as
surrounding text with the <STRIKE>...</STRIKE> HTML
tag pair.

sub

Use the sub() method of the String object to display text as subscript. Using this method yields the same result as surrounding text with the HTML tag pair _{...}.

Syntax:

string.sub()

Example:

document.write("H" + "2".sub() + "O = water")

submit

Use the submit() method of the form object to submit a form (that is, to send it for processing to the server program specified in the ACTION attribute, which is defined as part of the <FORM>...</FORM> tag pair).

Syntax:

formName.submit()

Example:

document.myForm.submit()

substring

Use the substring() method of the String object to return a *substring* (or portion) of a specified string.

Remember that the first character of a string has index 0, not 1; so when you supply an index range of (2, 4), you're actually asking for the third and fourth characters of the string to be returned to you. Why not the third through the fifth characters? Because substring() *stops one character before* the second index you give it.

Syntax:

string.substring(indexA, indexB)

Example:

The following example displays the string "Woman":

document.write("Wonder Woman".substring(7, 12))

W o n d e r **W o m a n**

0 1 2 3 4 5 6 **7 8 9 10 11**

Hey, so it's not very intuitive until you see the indexed string all laid out, — but it works! If you do a great deal of text manipulation, you can get the hang of it in no time.

sup

Use the sup() method of the String object to display text as superscript. Using this method yields the same result as surrounding text with the HTML tag pair ^{...}.

Syntax:

```
string.sup()
```

Example:

```
document.write("Scooter's Better-Than-Homemade
    Cinnamon Rolls" + "TM".sup())
```

tan

Use the tan() method of the Math object to return the tangent of a number.

Syntax:

```
Math.tan(number)
```

Example:

```
var myTangent = Math.tan(1)
```

toGMTString

Use the toGMTString() method of the Date object to convert a date to a string. This method uses the Internet GMT conventions (which means that the time is returned in Greenwich Mean Time), and the format of the result that returns is slightly platform-dependent. Under Windows 95, for example, you get a string similar to the following:

```
Thu, 27 Jun 1996 16:51:24 GMT
```

Syntax:

```
dateObjectName.toGMTString()
```

Example:

```
var today = new Date() // gets today's date
var myDateString = today.toGMTString()
```

toLocaleString

Use the `toLocaleString()` method of the `Date` object to convert a date to a string that is based on local time. This method returns the correct local time, but the result is platform-dependent. On Windows 95, you get a string similar to the following:

`06/27/96 10:51:24`

Syntax:

`dateObjectName.toLocaleString()`

Example:

```
var today = new Date() // gets today's date
var myDateString = today.toLocaleString()
```

Every time that you hear the words *platform dependent,* your skin should begin to crawl and your limbs should start to twitch uncontrollably. Platform dependence is to be avoided whenever possible because it means that you either have to redo work (yuck!) or limit your audience to people running the same platform as you (double yuck!).

Sometimes you have no way around platform dependence; but, for dates, you can try to use the `getMonth()`, `getYear()`, and other such methods before you resort to the `toGMTString()` and `toLocaleString()` methods.

toLowerCase

Use the `toLowerCase()` method of the `string` object to convert a specified string to lowercase.

Syntax:

`string.toLowerCase()`

Example:

```
document.write("DON\'T SHOUT, I CAN HEAR YOU JUST
    FINE".toLowerCase())
```

toString

Every JavaScript object supports the `toString()` method. Use this method to represent any object as a string. If the object doesn't have a string value, `toString()`returns a string containing the type of the object. For example, `window.toString()` returns the string `"[object Window]"`.

Syntax:

```
object.toString()
```

Example:

```
document.write(document.lastModified.toString())
document.write(myFunction.toString())
document.write(myAge.toString())
document.write(Array.toString())
```

toUpperCase

Use the `toUpperCase()` method of the `String` object to convert a specified string to all uppercase.

Syntax:

```
string.toUpperCase()
```

Example:

```
document.write("could you please speak
    up?".toUpperCase())
```

UTC

Use the `UTC()` method of the `Date` object to return the number of milliseconds between a specified date and January 1, 1970, 00:00:00. (*UTC* stands for Universal Coordinated Time, and it's basically the same thing as GMT.) Remember that, because this is GMT, any difference between your local time and GMT is reflected in the return value. For example, if 6 hours are between your local time and GMT and you put in a value of hours as *0,* the return value has hours set to *6.*

Syntax:

```
Date.UTC(year, month, day [, hours] [, minutes] [,
    seconds])
```

Example:

```
GMTDate = new Date(Date.UTC(96, 7, 24, 0, 0, 0))
```

write

Use the `write()` method of the `document` object to write expressions to the specified document.

You can use the `write()` method not only within the `<SCRIPT>...</SCRIPT>` tags, but within event handlers, as well. For example, this statement is perfectly legal: `onClick="anotherWindow.document.write('You clicked it!')"`.

Of course, you can't write to the current document in the current window in an event handler because the document has already been displayed.

Syntax:

```
write(expression1 [, expression2] ... [,
    expressionN])
```

Example:

```
document.write("Here is the monthly sales total: " +
    monthlyTotal)
```

writeln

Use the `writeln()` method of the `document` object to write any number of expressions to the specified document. Although `writeln()` appends a newline character (the HTML equivalent of a carriage return) to the end of the displayed expressions, unless you use the newline character within an HTML tag pair that cares (like `<PRE>...</PRE>`, which preformats text), the display is identical to that of `write()`.

Syntax:

```
writeln(expression1 [, expression2] ... [,
    expressionN])
```

Example:

```
document.writeln("<PRE>")
document.writeln("moogoo")
document.writeln("gaipan")
document.writeln("</PRE>")
```

Part VII

Properties (Object Data)

If you're familiar with object-oriented concepts, you know that every object, by definition, is made up of two things:

- ✦ Data (implemented as properties)
- ✦ Behavior (implemented as methods)

Part VI is devoted to methods, which represent the behaviors associated with an object; this part describes properties — the items that represent an object's data.

In this part . . .

✔ **Accessing object properties**

✔ **Modifying object properties**

✔ **Relating object properties to their corresponding HTML tag attributes**

About Properties

In object-oriented terms, *properties* are values that describe objects. For instance, a dog object might have the following properties: color, weight, whether or not it's pedigreed, and so on.

You, the JavaScript author, set many of the properties that you see in this section when you define your objects in HTML. Unfortunately, the names of properties aren't always identical to the names of the attributes you set them to. For example, you may define ALINK="cornflowerblue" in your <BODY>...</BODY> tag, but you retrieve the value this way: document.alinkColor.

Three properties — name, value, and length — are presented a little differently than the other properties. Just about every object contains these three properties, and their values are very similar: form.name refers to the form's name, document.name refers to the document's name, textarea.value refers to a textarea object's value, and so on. So, I list these properties with no qualifiers (for instance, just plain value instead of document.form. textarea.value). Under their headings, you find a list of all the objects that support these properties and other useful stuff, like which HTML tag attribute an object property corresponds to.

action

Use the action property of the form object to access the value of the HTML ACTION attribute. This value represents the URL (usually a CGI program or a mailto: URL) that the form is sent to when the user clicks the Submit button. You can change the value for this property.

document.myForm.action

The Microsoft Internet Explorer doesn't support a value of mailto: for the form's ACTION attribute at the time of this writing.

alinkColor

Use the alinkColor property of the document object to access the value of the ALINK attribute. The value of ALINK represents the color that link text turns when a user *activates,* or clicks on, the link. Valid values for this property include hexadecimal RGB triplets (such as "00FFFFFF") and predefined strings (such as "red"), as shown in Appendix B. You can change the value for this property.

document.alinkColor

appCodeName

Use the `appCodeName` property of the `navigator` object to access the code name of the version of Navigator currently in use. This property is a read-only property — you can't change it.

```
navigator.appCodeName
```

applets

The `applets` array of the `document` object contains entries for each of the applets currently loaded in a page.

```
document.applets[0]
document.applets.length
```

appName

Use the `appName` property of the `navigator` object to access the name of the browser currently in use. You can't change the value for this property.

```
navigator.appName
```

appVersion

Use the `appVersion` property of the `navigator` object to access the version of the browser currently in use. This property is a read-only property.

```
navigator.appVersion
```

arguments

The `arguments` array is a property of the `function` object. The elements of the `arguments` array correspond to all the arguments defined for a particular `function` object.

```
myFunctionName.arguments[0]
myFunctionName.arguments.length
```

At the time of this writing, Navigator 3.0 does not support the `function.arguments` property.

bgColor

Use the bgColor property of the document object to access the value of the BGCOLOR attribute defined within the <BODY>... </BODY> tag pair. The value of bgColor represents the color of the entire document background, which you can easily change.

```
document.bgColor
```

border

Use the border property of the image object to access or change the size of an embedded image's border (in pixels).

```
document.myImage.border
```

checked (checkbox)

Use the checked property of the checkbox object to see whether your user has checked a check box (clicked it on) or not (clicked it off). The value for the checked property always returns either *true* (for checked) or *false* (meaning unchecked). You can change the value of this property.

```
document.myForm.myCheckbox.checked
```

checked (radio)

Use the checked property of the radio object to see whether your user has set a radio button (clicked it on) or not (clicked it off). The value for the checked property always returns either *true* (for set) or *false* (not set). You can change the value of this property.

```
document.myForm.myRadioButton[0].checked
```

complete

Use the complete property of the image object to find out whether a user's Web browser has completed its attempt to load an image.

```
document.images[0].complete
```

cookie

A `cookie` is a property of the `document` object. The value can be any string value (except no white space, semicolons, or commas are allowed). A JavaScript statement can change this property.

```
document.cookie
```

defaultChecked (checkbox)

Use the `defaultChecked` property of the `checkbox` object to see whether a check box was initially defaulted to *selected.* The value for the `defaultChecked` property always returns either *true* (meaning that the `defaultChecked` property was initially defaulted to *on*) or *false* (meaning that it wasn't). You can change the value of this property to override the default setting.

```
document.myForm.myCheckbox.defaultChecked
```

defaultChecked (radio)

Use the `defaultChecked` property of the `radio` object to see whether a radio button was initially defaulted to *selected.* The value for the `defaultChecked` property always returns either *true* (meaning that the `defaultChecked` property was initially defaulted to *on*) or *false* (meaning that it wasn't). You can change the value of this property to override the default setting.

```
document.myForm.myRadioButton[0].defaultChecked
```

defaultSelected

Use the `defaultSelected` property of the `option` object to see whether a selected option was selected by default (value is *true*) or not (value is *false*). You can change the value of this property.

```
document.myForm.selectMusic.options[0].defaultSelected
```

defaultStatus

Use the `defaultStatus` property of the `window` object to access the default message that appears in a window's status bar. You can change the value for this property.

```
window.defaultStatus
```

defaultValue (password)

Use the defaultValue value of the password object to see the initially-defined default password value.

```
document.myForm.myPassword.defaultValue
```

defaultValue (text)

Use the defaultValue property of the text object to access the value of the VALUE attribute of a text object. You can change the value for this property.

```
document.myForm.myTextField.defaultValue
```

defaultValue (textarea)

Use the defaultValue property of the textarea object to access the contents of the textToDisplay textarea attribute. You can change the value for this property.

```
document.myForm.myTextareaField.defaultValue
```

description

The description property is associated with both the mimeTypes object and the plugins object. When associated with the mimeTypes object, the description property represents a description of a MIME type. When associated with the plugins object, description represents a description of a plug-in.

```
navigator.mimeTypes[0].description
navigator.plugins[0].description
```

E

The E property of the Math object represents Euler's mathematical constant and the base of natural logarithms This property is read-only.

```
Math.E
```

elements

The elements array is associated with the form object — the elements array enables you to access all the elements that have been defined for a form (button, checkbox, hidden, password, radio, reset, select, submit, text, and textarea). The array is in *source code order* (the first element defined is the 0th element in the array, and so forth). Elements in the array are read-only.

```
document.myForm.elements[0]
document.myForm.elements.length
```

embeds

The embeds array associated with the document object enables you to access all the plug-ins loaded into your Web page. Each element in the embeds array corresponds to an element defined with the HTML tag <EMBED>.

```
document.embeds[0]
document.embeds.length
```

enabledPlugin

Use the enabledPlugin property of the mimeTypes object to access the plugins object that handles the corresponding MIME type (see navigator.mimeTypes.type).

```
navigator.mimeTypes[0].enabledPlugin
```

encoding

Use the encoding property of the form object to access the ENCTYPE form attribute. The value is one of the following two strings: application/x-www-form-urlencoded, which is the default value, or multipart/form-data. You can change the value for this property.

```
document.myForm.encoding
```

fgColor

The fgColor property of the document object describes the color of the text displayed in a document. The fgColor property corresponds to the TEXT attribute defined as part of the <BODY>...</BODY> tag pair. You can change the value for this property, but values must be either hexadecimal RGB triplets or predefined strings. ***See also*** Appendix B.

```
document.fgColor
```

filename

Use the `filename` property of the `plugins` object to access the name of the plug-in executable file on disk.

```
navigator.plugins[0].filename
navigator.plugins["pluginName"].filename
```

forms

The `forms` array associated with the `document` object enables you to access all the forms that have been defined for a document. The `forms` array is in *source code order* (the first form defined is the first element in the array (`[0]`), and so forth). Elements of the `forms` array are read-only.

```
document.forms[0]
document.forms.length
```

frames

The `frames` array of the `window` object enables you to access all the `frame` objects associated with a window. The `frames` array of the `window` object contains an entry for each frame object defined with the `<FRAME>` tag inside a `<FRAMESET>` tag (such frame objects are also called *child frames*), in the order they appear in the source code. Elements of the `frames` array are read-only.

```
frames[0]
frames.length
```

hash

The `hash` property is associated with the `area`, `link`, and `location` objects. In all these objects, the `hash` property references one little piece of the overall `href` property belonging to each object. The `href` property contains an entire URL; the `hash` property contains the piece of that URL that represents an anchor name. (The hash property is named hash because anchor names are always preceded by a hash symbol (#), like this: "#TOC".)

You can change the value for this property.

```
// syntax for link object as well as area object
document.links[index].hash

location.hash
```

height

The height property of the image object lets you access the value of the HEIGHT attribute of the HTML <IMG> tag. A valid value for the height property can either be an integer (measured in pixels), or a percentage (expressing a percent of total window height). The value for this property is read-only.

```
document.myImage.height
```

host

The host property is associated with the area, link, and location objects. Use the host property of each object to access the hostname:port portion of a URL. A valid value for the host property must be a string representing a hostname and a port, separated by a colon (:).

A port, or more correctly, a *port address,* tells your browser exactly what software process on a server the browser should talk to when it loads a URL. In practice, ports are often predefined, so you may never have occasion to worry about specifying a port name.

You can change the value for this property.

```
// syntax for link object as well as area object
document.links[index].host

location.host
```

hostname

The hostname property is associated with the area, link, and location objects. The hostname property of each object refers to the host and domain name of a network host. A valid value for the hostname property is a string similar to the following: austin.ibm.com. You can change the value for the hostname property.

```
// syntax for link object as well as area object
document.links[index].hostname

location.hostname
```

href

The href property is associated with the area, link, and location objects. The href property of each object enables you to access a string that represents the entire URL for that object.

You can change the value for this property. An example of a valid value is `http://software.ibm.com`.

```
// syntax for link object as well as area object
document.links[index].href
```

```
location.href
```

 Be aware that the `href` property is comprised of several other properties (`hash`, `host`, `hostname`, `port`, and `search`). That means that if you change the values of any of these other properties, you're also indirectly changing the value of `href`.

hspace

The `hspace` property of the `image` object enables you to access the value of the `HSPACE` attribute of the HTML `<IMG>` tag. This value specifies a margin (measured in pixels) between the left and right edges of an image and the surrounding screen real estate. The `hspace` property only applies to images that have `"left"` or `"right"` defined for the value of the `ALIGN` attribute of the `<IMG>` tag.

```
document.myImage.hspace
```

images

The `images` array associated with the `document` object enables you to access all the images loaded into your page. Each element in the `images` array corresponds to an element defined with the HTML tag `<IMG>`.

```
document.images[0]
document.images.length
```

index

The `index` property of the `option` object enables you to access the position of an `option` in a `select` object. Values for the `index` property are integers, beginning with zero, and are read-only.

```
document.myForm.mySelectField.options[0].index
```

lastModified

Access the `lastModified` property of the `document` object to determine when a document was last modified. The value for this property is a string, and it's read-only.

```
document.lastModified
```

length

The `length` property is used on several different objects and arrays, and its value is always read-only.

Object	*Usage*	*Value*
`array`	`myArray.length`	Number of array elements
`form`	`document.myForm.length`	Number of elements for a form
`frame`	`myFrame.length`	Number of child frames within a frame
`history`	`history.length`	Number of entries in the `history` object
`radio`	`document.myForm.myRadio.length`	Number of radio buttons in a `radio` object
`select`	`document.myForm.mySelect.length`	Number of options in a `select` object
`string`	`document.myForm.myString.length`	Number of characters in a string
`window`	`length`	Number of frames within a window

Array	*Usage*	*Value*
`anchors`	`document.anchors.length`	Number of anchors in a document
`elements`	`document.myForm.elements.length`	Number of elements defined for a form
`embeds`	`document.myForm.embeds.length`	Number of embedded plug-ins
`forms`	`document.forms.length`	Number of forms defined in a document
`frames`	`frames.length`	Number of frames in a frame/window
`images`	`document.images.length`	Number of images in a document
`links`	`document.links.length`	Number of links in a document
`options`	`document.myForm.mySelect.options.length`	Number of options in a `select` object

Surprise! Even though `anchors` is an array and its elements are purportedly in source code order (that is, the 0th element corresponds to the first anchor defined in a file, the first

element to the second anchor defined, and so on), the value of
`document.anchors[index]` is *always null* (*null* is geekspeak
for "never existed"). What a sense of humor those JavaScript
architects had, huh?

linkColor

Use the `linkColor` property of the `document` object to access
the value of the `LINK` attribute. This value represents the color of
initially displayed link text. Valid values for this property include
hexadecimal RGB triplets (such as `"00FFFFFF"`) and predefined
strings (such as `"red"`). You can change the values for this
property. *See also* Appendix B.

```
document.linkColor
```

links

The `links` array of the `document` object enables you to access all
the links that have been defined for a document. The array is in
source code order (the first link defined is the 0th element in the
array, and so forth). Elements of the array are read-only.

```
document.links[0]
document.links.length
```

LN2

The `LN2` property of the `Math` object represents the natural
logarithm of the number *2* (approximately 0.693). This property is
read-only. (Unless you're a heavy-duty math person, my guess is
you'll never feel the urge to use `LN2` in your JavaScript calculations — but please feel free!)

```
Math.LN2
```

LN10

The `LN10` property of the `Math` object represents the natural
logarithm of 10 (approximately 2.302). This property is read-only.

```
Math.LN10
```

location

Use the location property of the document object to access a document's complete URL. The value for this property is read-only.

`document.location`

LOG2E

The LOG2E property of the Math object represents the base 2 logarithm (approximately 1.442). This property is read-only.

`Math.LOG2E`

LOG10E

The LOG10E property of the Math object represents the base 10 logarithm (approximately 0.434). Because the base 10 logarithm is a mathematical constant, this property is read-only.

`Math.LOG10E`

lowsrc

The lowsrc property of the image object reflects the value of the LOWSRC attribute defined as part of the HTML <IMG> tag. A valid value for this property is a URL for a low-resolution version of the image to load.

`document.myImage.lowsrc`

method

The method property of the form object enables you to access the value for the METHOD attribute defined as part of the <FORM>...</FORM> tag pair. A valid value for this property is a string that specifies how form field input is sent to the server when the form is submitted (either "GET" or "POST").

Take a look at Chapter 10 of *JavaScript For Dummies* (by Yours Truly) for a complete discussion of the difference between setting this property equal to "GET" and to "POST".

`document.myForm.method`

mimeTypes

The `mimeTypes` array associated with the `navigator` object enables you to access all the MIME types supported by the client (whether defined internally, by helper applications, or by plug-ins). Each element in the `mimeTypes` array is a `mimeTypes` object.

```
navigator.mimeTypes[0]
```

name

The `name` property is available on many different objects. Unless otherwise noted, the `name` property always represents the NAME attribute for an object.

Object	Usage	Comments
applet	document.applets[0].name	
button	document.myForm.myButton.name	
checkbox	document.myForm.myCheckbox.name	
fileUpload	document.myForm.myFileUpload.name	
frame	myFrame.name	
hidden	document.myForm.myHidden.name	
image	document.myForm.myImage.name	
password	document.myForm.myPassword.name	
plugin	document.embeds[0].name	
radio	document.myForm.myRadio[0].name	All radio buttons in a set have the same name.
reset	document.myForm.myReset.name	
select	document.myForm.mySelect.name	
submit	document.myForm.mySubmit.name	
text	document.myForm.myText.name	
textarea	document.myForm.myTextarea.name	
window	window.name	window.name is read-only; its value is that of the windowVar attribute.
options array	document.myForm.mySelect.options[0].name	

Nothing particularly special applies to the implementation of radio buttons. *Any* group of form objects to which you give the same name is automatically organized in an array.

opener

When you open a window using the `open()` method, you can use the `opener` property of the `window` object to access the window of the calling document.

```
windowReference.opener
```

At the time of this writing, Internet Explorer 3.0 doesn't support the `window.opener` property.

options

The `options` array, associated with the `select` object, enables you to access all the options that have been defined for a `select` object. The array is in source code order (the first option defined is the 0th element in the array, and so forth). Elements of the array are read-only.

```
document.myForm.selectFieldName.options[0]
document.myForm.selectFieldName.options.length
```

parent (frame)

The `parent` property of the `frame` object is a synonym for a frame whose frameset contains the current frame (the frame you're in when you're referencing the `parent` property). When the parent is a frame, the value for the `parent` property is the value of the NAME attribute defined as part of the `<FRAME>...</FRAME>` declaration. When the parent is a window, the value for the parent property is an internal reference. (That is, you can use the internal reference to refer to the properties of the window, but the internal reference is not much to look at.) The value for the `parent` property is read-only.

```
parent
```

parent (window)

The `parent` property of the `window` object is a synonym for a frame whose frameset contains the current window (the window you're in when you're referencing the `parent` property). When the parent is a frame, the value for the `parent` property is the value of the `NAME` attribute defined as part of the `<FRAME>...</FRAME>` declaration. When the parent is a window, the value for the parent property is an internal reference. (That is, you can use the internal reference to refer to the properties of the window, but the internal reference is not much to look at.) The value for the `parent` property is read-only.

```
parent
```

pathname

The `pathname` property is associated with the `area`, `link`, and `location` objects. Use the `pathname` property of each object to access the path portion of that object's URL. You can set the string value for the `pathname` property.

```
// syntax for both link object and area object
document.links[index].pathname

document.location.pathname
```

PI

`PI`, a property of the `Math` object, refers to the mathematical constant for the ratio of the circumference of a circle to its diameter (approximately 3.1415). The value for `PI` is read-only.

```
Math.PI
```

plugins

The `plugins` array associated with the `navigator` object enables you to access all the plug-ins (`plugin` objects) currently installed on the client. Each element in the `plugins` array is a `plugin` object.

```
navigator.plugins[0]
```

port

The `port` property is associated with the `area`, `link`, and `location` objects. The `port` property of each object is a *substring,* or piece, of that object's `host` property (which is itself a substring of that object's `href` property). The `port` property is the piece of the `host` after the colon.

```
// syntax is for link object as well as area object
document.links[0].port
```

```
location.port
```

 For a given href, if no value appears for port and the value of protocol is http://, the server assumes a default port value of 80, which is the default port for all Web-type communications.

protocol

The protocol property is associated with the area, link, and location objects. Use the protocol property to access a substring of the object's URL, beginning with the first character and ending with the first colon. (A common value for protocol is http://.). You can change the protocol property's value.

```
// syntax is for both link and area objects
document.links[0].protocol
```

```
location.protocol
```

prototype

The prototype property is available for any object that's created with the new operator, as shown in the following table. Use the prototype property to add your own custom properties to whole types of objects:

```
// custom property called "description" is defined
// for all date objects
Date.prototype.description = null
```

```
// a new date variable is created, called "today"
today = new Date()
```

```
// the new description property is assigned a value
today.description="Today is my birthday!"
```

Data Type	Usage
Array	Array.prototype.newPropertyName = null
Date	Date.prototype.newPropertyName = null
Function	Function.prototype.newPropertyName = null
Option	Option.prototype.newPropertyName = null
String	String.prototype.newPropertyName = null
Any user-defined object	Animal.prototype.newPropertyName = null

referrer

When a user loads a linked document, the referrer property of that document holds the value for the URL of the calling document. The value for referrer is read-only.

```
document.referrer
```

search (link)

Used the search property of the link object to access the portion of the link URL that contains query information (that is, form input fields sent to a CGI program to be used for a document-based database search). A valid search value is a string that begins with a question mark (?) followed by any number of attribute-value pairs, each separated by an ampersand (&). You can change the value for search.

```
document.links[0].search
```

search (location)

The search property of the location object is used to access the portion of the location URL that contains query information (that is, form input fields sent to a CGI program to be used for a document-based search of a database). A valid search value is a string that begins with a question mark (?) followed by any number of attribute-value pairs, each separated by an ampersand (&). You can change the value for search.

```
document.location.search
```

Try out any of the popular Web search engines, such as Yahoo!, AltaVista, or Excite, and you can see the value of the search property being sent to the respective CGI programs — right there in either Navigator's Location: window or Internet Explorer's Address window. For instance, when I asked the AltaVista search engine to fetch all the JavaScript-related Web pages it could find, here's what appeared in my Location: window:

```
http://www.altavista.digital.com/cgi-bin/
    query?pg=q&what=web&fmt=.&q=JavaScript
```

selected

Use the selected property of the option object to access a Boolean (true or false) value that describes whether an option in a selection has been selected. You can change the value of the selected property.

```
document.myForm.mySelectField.options[0].selected
```

selectedIndex (options)

Use the selectedIndex property of the options array to access the index of a selected option (an integer from 0 to however many options exist). If multiple options have been selected, the value of selectedIndex contains a reference only to the index of the very first option selected. The value for options.selectedIndex is the same as for select.selectedIndex, and you can change the value.

```
document.myForm.mySelectField.options.selectedIndex
```

selectedIndex (select)

Use the selectedIndex value to access the index of a select object. If multiple options have been selected, the value of selectedIndex contains a reference only to the index of the very first option selected. The value for select.selectedIndex is the same as for options.selectedIndex, and you can change the value.

```
document.myForm.mySelectField.selectedIndex
```

self (frame)

The self property of the frame object is a synonym for the current frame. (Gee, and all those philosophers spent so much time searching for the meaning of *self!* If only they had coded JavaScript!) The value for self is read-only.

```
self
```

self (window)

The self property of the window object is a synonym for the current window. The value for self is read-only.

```
self
```

SQRT1_2

The SQRT1_2 property of the Math object represents the mathematical constant for the square root of $^1/_2$ (approximately .707). Its value can't be changed.

```
Math.SQRT1_2
```

SQRT2

The SQRT2 property of the Math object represents the mathematical constant for the square root of two (approximately 1.414). Its value can't be changed.

```
Math.SQRT2
```

src

The src property of the image object reflects the value of the SRC attribute defined as part of the HTML <IMG> tag. A valid value for this property is a URL for the image to be loaded.

```
document.myImage.src
```

status

The status property of the window object contains a text value that appears in the window's status bar. You can change the status property's value.

```
status
```

The status property is different from the defaultStatus property. The value of the defaultStatus property is displayed in the status bar when nothing else is going on. In contrast, the value of the status property is displayed for a specific reason — for example, in response to an onMouseOver event (*see also* Part VIII, "Event Handlers," for more on events).

suffixes

The value for the suffixes property of the mimeTypes array represents a string listing, separated by commas, of all possible file suffixes (file suffixes are sometimes called *file extensions*) available for each corresponding MIME type.

```
navigator.mimeTypes[0].suffixes
```

target (form)

Use the `target` property of a `form` to access a string that specifies the window in which you want to receive responses from the server. The value for `form.target` is initially defined by the `TARGET` attribute as part of the `<FORM>...</FORM>` tag pair, but you can change it.

```
document.myForm.target
```

target (link, area)

Use the `target` property of a `link` or `area` object to access a string that identifies the name of the window a linked (or area mapped) document should be loaded into. The string value for `link.target` is initially defined by the `TARGET` attribute of the `<A>...</A>` tag pair, and the string value for `area.target` is initially defined by the `TARGET` attribute of the `<AREA>` tag; you can change the values for both if you wish.

```
// same syntax for both link and area objects
document.links[0].target
```

text

Use the `text` property of the `option` object to access the text that follows an `<OPTION>` tag that is defined as part of a `select` object. You can change the value for this object.

```
document.myForm.mySelectField.options[0].text
```

At the time of this writing, the `options[0].text` property is read-only in Internet Explorer 3.0.

title

The `title` property of the `document` object enables you to access the title of a document (the text that is defined between the `<TITLE>...</TITLE>` tag pair). The `title` property's value is read-only. For example:

```
<HEAD><TITLE>
Welcome to Bertram's Beanie Emporium
</TITLE></HEAD>
```

top

The top property of the window object refers to the topmost window that contains frames or nested framesets. Its value is read-only.

```
top
```

type

The type property is available on many different objects. The type property represents the HTML TYPE attribute for an object.

At the time of this writing, only Netscape Navigator Version 3.0 supports the type property.

Object	Usage	Return Value
button	document.myForm.myButton.type	"button"
checkbox	document.myForm.myCheckbox.type	"checkbox"
fileUpload	document.myForm.myFile.type	"file"
hidden	document.myForm.myHidden.type	"hidden"
password	document.myForm.myPassword.type	"password"
radio	document.myForm.myRadio[0].type	"radio"
reset	document.myForm.myReset.type	"reset"
select	document.myForm.mySelect.type	"select-one", "select-multiple" (MULTIPLE)
submit	document.myForm.mySubmit.type	"submit"
text	document.myForm.myText.type	"text"
textarea	document.myForm.myTextarea.type	"textarea"

type (mimeTypes)

The type property of the mimeTypes array, instead of representing the HTML TYPE attribute the way it does for all of the other objects, represents one of the MIME types supported by a browser session. *See also* the mimeTypes property described earlier in this part.

```
navigator.mimeTypes[0].type
```

userAgent

The userAgent property of the navigator object enables you to access a string value that represents the user-agent header (some computer-to-computer chit-chat that's roughly equivalent to "Hey, it's me again, the machine at port 123.456.7890"). Navigator automatically sends a user-agent header each time a form is submitted from a client browser to a server. Servers use this value to identify the client that's making a request; it's read-only.

```
navigator.userAgent
```

value

The value property represents a string that's associated with the value of whatever object you're trying to access.

Object	Usage	Comments
button	document.myForm.myButton.value	Read-only value is displayed on button face
checkbox	document.myForm.myCheckbox.value	Value is sent to server when checkbox is clicked (default is "on")
fileUpload	document.myForm.myFileUpload.value	Reflects the value selected by a user
hidden	document.myForm.myHidden.value	Initially reflects the VALUE attribute
option	document.myForm.mySelect.options[0].value	Value is sent to server when option is selected
password	document.myForm.myPassword.value	Initially reflects the VALUE attribute
radio	document.myForm.myRadio[0].value	Value is sent to server when checkbox is clicked (default is "on")
reset	document.myForm.myReset.value	Read-only value is displayed on button face; default is "Reset"
submit	document.myForm.mySubmit.value	Read-only value is displayed on button face; default is "Submit Query"
text	document.myForm.myText.value	Initially reflects the VALUE attribute
textarea	document.myForm.myTextarea.value	Initially reflects the VALUE attribute
options array	document.myForm.mySelect.options[0].value	Value is sent to server when option is selected

vlinkColor

The `vlinkColor` property enables you to access the value defined by the `VLINK` attribute declared as part of the `<BODY>...</BODY>` tag pair. The `vlinkColor` property defines the color of a clicked-on, or followed, link. You can change the value for the `VLINK` attribute to a hexadecimal RGB triplet or to a predefined color string that corresponds to such a triplet.

```
document.vlinkColor
```

vspace

The `vspace` property of the `image` object enables you to access the value of the `VSPACE` attribute of the HTML `<IMG>` tag. This value specifies a margin (measured in pixels) between the top and bottom edges of an image and the surrounding screen real estate. This property only applies to images that have "left" or "right" defined for the value of the `ALIGN` attribute of the `<IMG>` tag.

```
document.myImage.vspace
```

width

The `width` property of the `image` object lets you access the value of the `WIDTH` attribute of the HTML `<IMG>` tag. A valid value for the `width` property can be either an integer (measured in pixels), or a percentage (expressing a percent of total window width). The value for this property is read-only.

```
document.myImage.width
```

window

The `window` property is a synonym for the current window (or current frame, because frames *are* windows). The value for this property is read-only, and it's also the same as the `self` property of the `window` object.

Part VIII

Event Handlers

An *event handler* is a piece of code attached to some object that a Web user may interact with, like a push button, a link, a text field, and so on. When the user falls into your JavaScript-powered little Web page and does something like "clicking on a Submit button," the event handler executes some JavaScript instructions associated with that user's action. For example, when the user rolls the mouse pointer over a hypertext link, an event handler runs some code that make the URL appear in the Web browser's status bar.

This part shows you the various JavaScript event handlers that you can use in your HTML code to make your Web page more interactive and intuitive to users who visit your Web site.

In this part . . .

- ✔ **Getting familiar with the different event handlers**
- ✔ **Understanding event handler syntax**
- ✔ **Calling event handlers**

About Events

In JavaScript, *event* refers to some action (usually user-initiated) that affects an HTML form element. Some examples of user-initiated events include

✦ Clicking (affects push buttons and radio buttons)

✦ Checking (affects check boxes)

✦ Selecting (affects text elements and list boxes)

✦ Changing a value (affects text elements)

You use an *event handler* to have the browser invoke a set of JavaScript statements automatically whenever the associated event occurs.

In Navigator 3.0, you can reset the function initially assigned to an event handler in an HTML statement by using a JavaScript statement. The following code snippet is an example of how you can reset the value of onBlur to a new function called someOtherFunction():

```
document.myForm.lastName.onblur="someOtherFunction"
```

Notice the lack of parentheses in the preceding assignment? (It's not someOtherFunction(), it's someOtherFunction.) When you reset the value for an event handler, you have to leave off the parentheses. Trust me, you don't want to know why.

onAbort

The onAbort event handler is associated with the Image object and can be used to trigger the execution of some JavaScript code each time users *abort,* or stop loading, an image in a Web page. Users can abort an image load by clicking the Stop button on their Web browsers while the image is loading (which they typically do if the image is so large that they become impatient).

Syntax:

```
onAbort="event handling text"
```

Example:

The onAbort event handler is only available on the Image object, as shown in the following code:

```
<IMG NAME="thistle" SRC="images/thistle.gif"
    onAbort="alert('You missed a great picture!')">
```

onBlur

onBlur is an event handler associated with the frame, select, text, textarea, and window objects. onBlur is invoked when an element *blurs,* or loses focus. Put another way, blurring occurs when a user clicks on one form element and then clicks on a new element, changing the focus from the first element (which is now blurred) to the new element (which is the focus of the next event, waiting to respond to user input).

 onBlur events on the select, text, and textarea objects provide a great opportunity to do any field-level validation that you need to do. The user presumably has finished entering text or making a selection, so if you invoke a function to validate the field at this point, you can get back to the user immediately if a problem exists. *See also* "Validating User Input" in Part IX.

Syntax:

```
onBlur="event handling text"
```

Example:

You can use the onBlur event handler with the frame, select, text, textarea, and window objects. The following sections contain examples of onBlur for each object.

frame

The first chunk of code below defines a frame named frame1 whose source is the HTML file framcon1.html; the second chunk of code shows how the onBlur event handler is implemented for frame1.

```
<FRAMESET ROWS="50%,50%" COLS="40%,60%">
<FRAME SRC="framcon1.html" NAME="frame1">
<FRAME SRC="framcon2.html" NAME="frame2">
</FRAMESET>
```

(The following code, which defines the frame frame1, is from the file called **framcon1.html** highlighted in the preceding code sample.)

```
<BODY BGCOLOR="lightgrey"
    onBlur="document.bgColor='black'"
onFocus="document.bgColor='white'">
```

select

```
<FORM>
Product: <SELECT NAME="productSelection" SIZE=1
onBlur="processSelection(this)">
<OPTION VALUE="shirt"> t-shirt
```

(continued)

(continued)

```
<OPTION VALUE="pen"> ball-point pen
<OPTION VALUE="weight"> monogrammed paperweight
</SELECT>
```

text

```
Last name: <INPUT TYPE="text" VALUE=""
    NAME="lastName" SIZE=25
    onBlur="verifyExistence(this.value)">
```

textarea

```
<TEXTAREA NAME="commentField" ROWS=5 COLS=50
onBlur="if (!this.value) { confirm('Are you sure
    you don't want to comment?')}">
</TEXTAREA>
</FORM>
```

window

```
<BODY BGCOLOR="lightgrey"
    onBlur="document.bgColor='black'"
onFocus="document.bgColor='white'">
```

When calling a function from an event handler, passing along a
copy of the object that's involved is a great idea. You can do this
by passing the this keyword; that way, you can keep your
function code generic enough to reuse over and over again.
This code fragment, repeated from an earlier section, shows an
example of this:

```
Last name: <INPUT TYPE="text" VALUE=""
    NAME="lastName" SIZE=25
    onBlur="verifyExistence(this.value)">
```

When a user blurs the lastName field, the JavaScript interpreter
calls the verifyExistence() function and passes it
this.value. Instead of having to know what form element value
to access in verifyExistence() (Yecch, hard coding! The root
of all evil!), all you have to do in verifyExistence() is work
with the generic value passed in.

onChange

The onChange event handler is similar to onBlur, except that
onChange is invoked only if some change has been made in the
value of a select, text, or textarea element, *in addition* to the
loss of focus. Depending on your application, sometimes you may
want to call the functions that do your field-level validation from
an onChange event handler instead of from onBlur. That way, a
value is verified only if it has changed, not just when a user moves

to a different area of the form. (Why go to all the trouble of revalidating a value if you know that the value hasn't changed since the *last* time that you validated it?) ***See also*** "Validating User Input" in Part IX.

Syntax:

```
onChange="event handling text"
```

Example:

You can use the onChange event handler with the select, text, and textarea form elements. The following sections contain examples of each event handler.

select

```
<FORM>
Product: <SELECT NAME="productSelection" SIZE=1
onChange="processSelection(this)">
<OPTION VALUE="keyring"> key ring
<OPTION VALUE="sweat"> sweatshirt
<OPTION VALUE="horn"> monogrammed shoehorn
</SELECT>
```

text

```
Last name: <INPUT TYPE="text" VALUE=""
    NAME="lastName" SIZE=25
    onChange="verifyExistence(this.value)">
```

textarea

```
<TEXTAREA NAME="commentField" ROWS=5 COLS=50
onChange="if (!this.value) { confirm('Are you sure
    you don't want to comment?')}">
 </TEXTAREA>
</FORM>
```

onClick

A user invokes the onClick event handler when the user clicks on a clickable form element.

Navigator 3.0 enables you to stop an onClick event if your event handler code returns false (0). For example, the following code snippet allows users to change their minds after they click on the link and stop the link URL from loading if they press the "Cancel" button displayed by the confirm() method. (***See also*** the "confirm" section in Part VI.)

```
<A HREF="http://www.dummies.com"
onClick="return confirm('Okay to go ahead and
    connect?')">
Dummies Press Homepage </A>
```

Internet Explorer 3.0 doesn't support this feature at the time of this writing.

Syntax:
```
onClick="event handling text"
```

Example:
You can use the `onClick` event handler with all the following form elements: `button`, `checkbox`, `link`, `radio`, `reset`, and `submit`. The following sections contain examples of each.

button
```
<INPUT TYPE="button" NAME="orderNow" VALUE="order"
onClick="tallyOrder()">
```

checkbox
```
<INPUT TYPE="checkbox" NAME="firstBook"
    VALUE="firstBook"
onClick="if (this.checked) { sendThankYouLetter()
                           }">
Is this your first ...For Dummies book purchase?
```

link
```
<A HREF=""
    onClick="this.href=pickURLBasedOnUserPreferences()"
> You'll want to see this!
```

radio
```
Which is your favorite vacation destination?
<INPUT TYPE="radio" NAME="vacationSelection"
    VALUE="beach"
onClick="displayPage('beachfront property')">
    The beach
<INPUT TYPE="radio" NAME="vacationSelection"
    VALUE="mountain"
onClick="displayPage('mountain cabins')">
    The mountains
<INPUT TYPE="radio" NAME="vacationSelection"
    VALUE="city"
onClick="displayPage('posh hotels')"> Anywhere I
    can get room service
```

reset
```
<INPUT TYPE="reset" NAME="reset" VALUE="Clear form"
onClick="resetCalculatedTotals()">
```

Netscape Navigator running on a Windows platform doesn't care if you return a value of `false` for a `reset` `onClick` event handler; it goes ahead and resets the form no matter what happens when a user clicks the reset button — even if you think you stopped the reset from happening in the `onClick` event handling code.

submit

```
<INPUT TYPE="submit" NAME="submit" VALUE="Submit
    form"
onClick="checkConsistency()">
```

onError

You can use the onError event handler to trigger the execution of some JavaScript code every time an error occurs while a user is attempting to load either an image (the Image object) or a document (the window object). A good use for the onError event handler is to invoke a custom function designed to examine the error, figure out what caused it, and then suggest solutions.

Syntax:

```
onError="event handler text"
```

Example:

You can use the onError event handler with both the Image and window objects. The following code shows examples of each.

Image

```
<IMG NAME="noSuchAnimal" SRC="dummy.gif"
onError="alert(document.myForm.noSuchAnimal.name +
    ' could not be loaded')">
```

window

```
window.onerror=myOnErrorHandler
function myOnErrorHandler(message, url, lineNumber)
    {
    ...
    return true
}
```

Don't want your users to see *any* JavaScript-generated errors for a particular document? You can head them all off at the pass before they're displayed to the user by setting the onError event handler equal to null, like this:

```
window.onerror = null
```

onFocus

onFocus is an event handler associated with the frame, select, text, textarea, and window objects. Think of this event handler as the anti-onBlur; instead of responding when an object *loses* focus, onFocus is invoked when an object *gains* focus. (An object gains focus when a user tabs to, or clicks on, the object.)

You might expect that selecting text in a text or textarea element would trigger the onFocus event handler because *selecting* text implies clicking on that text, which should (in turn) give focus to that element. Well, that conclusion is logical, but it's incorrect. JavaScript considers text selection within a field a special case; instead of calling the onFocus event handler, JavaScript invokes the onSelect event handler.

See also "onSelect," later in this part.

Guess what happens if the code that's invoked by the onFocus event handler contains a call to a dialog box ? Well, after the element gets focus, the dialog box pops up. The user clicks OK or Cancel or whatever. Focus returns to the element. The dialog box pops up. The user clicks OK or Cancel or whatever. Focus returns to the element. The dialog box pops up. . . . Can you say *endless loop?* Please, don't try this at home!

Syntax:

```
onFocus="event handler text"
```

Example:

You can use the onFocus event handler with the frame, select, text, textarea, and window objects. The following sections contain examples of each.

frame

The first section of code below defines a frame named frame1 whose source is the HTML file framcon1.html; the second section shows how the onFocus event handler is implemented for frame1.

```
<FRAMESET ROWS="50%,50%" COLS="40%,60%"
onLoad="display()">
<FRAME SRC="framcon1.html" NAME="frame1">
<FRAME SRC="framcon2.html" NAME="frame2">
</FRAMESET>
```

The following code fragment is found in the file called **framcon1.html** referenced in the preceding code.

```
<BODY BGCOLOR="lightgrey"
    onBlur="document.bgColor='black'"
onFocus="document.bgColor='white'">
```

select

```
<FORM>
Product: <SELECT NAME="productSelection" SIZE=1
onFocus="validateDependentFields()">
<OPTION VALUE="shirt"> t-shirt
<OPTION VALUE="mug"> mug
<OPTION VALUE="rag"> monogrammed dishrag
</SELECT>
```

text

```
Last name: <INPUT TYPE="text" VALUE=""

NAME="lastName" SIZE=25
onFocus="validateDependentFields()">
```

textarea

```
<TEXTAREA NAME="commentField" ROWS=5 COLS=50
onFocus="validateDependentFields()">
</TEXTAREA>
</FORM>
```

window

```
<BODY BGCOLOR="white"
onBlur="document.bgColor='orange'"
onFocus="document.bgColor='green'">
```

onLoad

The onLoad event handler is associated with both the window
(frame) object and the image object. You can use the onLoad
event handler of the window object in two ways:

✦ To trigger some JavaScript code immediately after a window
loads

✦ To trigger some JavaScript code immediately after all the
frames in a frameset load

If you define an onLoad event handler for both the window
(in the <BODY>...</BODY> tag pair) and for a frameset (in the
<FRAMESET>...</FRAMESET> tag pair), the onLoad event
handler associated with the window executes first, and *then* the
onLoad associated with the frameset executes.

onLoad gives you the opportunity to do any initialization necessary for your application — things that need to be done before the
user gets a crack at the page or the image. You may want to
display the current date and time, for example, or play a little
welcoming tune.

Syntax:

```
onLoad="event handler text"
```

Example:

You can use the `onLoad` event handler with either the `image` object or the `window` (`frame`) object. The following section contains examples of both types of event handlers.

image

```
<IMG NAME="thistle" SRC="images/thistle.gif"
    onLoad="beginAnimation(this)">
```

window

```
<BODY onLoad="displayCustomWelcome()">

<FRAMESET ROWS="50%,50%" COLS="40%,60%"
onLoad="initializeVariables()">
<FRAME SRC="frame1.html" NAME="frame1">
<FRAME SRC="frame2.html" NAME="frame2">
</FRAMESET>
```

onMouseOut

Use `onMouseOut` to recognize when a user moves the mouse pointer off a link or an area. One `onMouseOut` event is generated each time that a user moves a mouse from a `link` or `area` to someplace else on the form.

Syntax:

```
onMouseOut="event handler text"
```

Example:

`onMouseOut` is available for both the `Area` and `link` objects, as shown in the following examples.

area

```
<MAP NAME="thistleMap">
<AREA NAME="topThistle" COORDS="0,0,228,318"
    HREF="javascript:displayMessage()"
onMouseOver="self.status='When you see this mes-
    sage, click your left mouse button'; return
    true"
onMouseOut="self.status=''; return true">
</MAP>
```

link

```
<A HREF="http://home.netscape.com/"
    onMouseOut="status='Thanks for visiting; return
    true">
Netscape</A>
```

If you want to set the value for the status bar, as in this example, I remember to return a value of *true* in the last JavaScript statement in the handler — otherwise, the value won't appear in the status bar.

onMouseOver

Use onMouseOver to recognize when a user moves the mouse pointer over a link (or over an area). One onMouseOver event is generated each time that a user moves a mouse to the link or area from someplace else on the form.

You can use this event handler to display a custom message in the status bar at the bottom of a document (instead of the default message) when a user drags a mouse pointer over a link or area. JavaScript automatically changes the user's mouse pointer from an arrow into a little hand when the pointer is dragged over a link or an area.

Syntax:

```
onMouseOver="event handler text"
```

Example:

onMouseOver is an event handler of area and link objects. Examples of both types follow.

area

```
<MAP NAME="thistleMap">
<AREA NAME="topThistle" COORDS="0,0,228,318"
    HREF="javascript:displayMessage()"
onMouseOver="self.status='When you see this mes-
    sage, click your left mouse button'; return
    true"
onMouseOut="self.status=''; return true">
</MAP>
```

link

```
<A HREF="http://home.netscape.com/"
    onMouseOver="status='Visit Netscape'; return
    true">
Mystery Link</A>
```

If you want to set the value for the status bar, as in this example, remember to return a value of *true* in the last JavaScript statement in the handler. If you don't, the interpreter ignores you and the status bar displays the default value — the URL of that link.

onReset

Use the onReset event handler of the form object to trigger some
JavaScript code to execute each time that a user clicks a Reset
button on a form.

Syntax:

onReset="*event handler text*"

Example:

The onReset event handler is only available on the form object:

```
<FORM onReset="alert('The form values have been
    reset.')">
```

onSelect

Use onSelect to trigger some JavaScript code to execute each
time that a user *selects* (highlights with the mouse) some part of
the text displayed in either a text or a textarea field.

Syntax:

onSelect="*event handler text*"

Example:

Use the onSelect event handler with either the text or the
textarea form elements. The following sections show examples
of each.

text

```
Last name: <INPUT TYPE="text" VALUE=""
    NAME="lastName" SIZE=25 onSelect="showHelp()">
```

textarea

```
<TEXTAREA NAME="commentField" ROWS=5 COLS=50
onSelect="showHelp()">
</TEXTAREA>
</FORM>
```

In both the preceding examples, the function showHelp() is
supposed to be called by the onSelect event handler when a user
selects any text contained either in the lastName field or the
commentField field. Unfortunately, it isn't! Netscape Navigator
3.0 (and earlier), as well as some early versions of Internet
Explorer, ignores the onSelect event handler.

onSubmit

Use the onSubmit event handler of the form object to gain more control over the form-submission process. When you use a Submit object (a button that automatically submits a form when a user clicks on it), you have no way to keep the form from being submitted after the button has been clicked — even if you return *false* to the Submit object's onClick event handler.

A way *does* exist to bail out at the last minute by using the onSubmit event handler instead. All you need to do is return a value of *false* to onSubmit if you don't want to go through with the submit, and a value of *true* if you do. Often the criterion you use to make your decision is the return value of a function whose job in life is to look at the input data in its entirety to see if it's complete enough to bother submitting to the server, such as the verifyFormData() method in the example code below.

The default return value for the onSubmit event handler is *true*, so if you forget to return a value explicitly, the form will always be sent.

Syntax:

```
onSubmit="event handler text"
```

Example:

```
...
function verifyFormData(incomingForm)
{
    if ( // all the relevant values of incomingForm
         // are valid based on some criteria you
         // define) {
       return true
    }
    else {
       return false
    }
}
...
...
form.onSubmit="return verifyFormData(this)"
```

onUnload

Just like its counterpart, onLoad, you can use the onUnload event handler associated with the window (frame) object in two ways: to trigger some JavaScript code immediately after a window has been unloaded (exited) or to trigger some JavaScript code immediately after all frames in a frameset have been unloaded.

If you define an onUnload for both the window (in the <BODY>...
</BODY> tag pair) and for a frameset (in the <FRAMESET>...
</FRAMESET> tag pair), the onUnload associated with the
window executes first, and *then* the onUnload associated with
the frameset executes.

Syntax:

onUnload="*event handler text*"

Example:

<BODY onUnload="cleanUp()">

<FRAMESET ROWS="50%,50%" COLS="40%,60%"
onUnload="cleanUpFrameData()">
<FRAME SRC="frame1.html" NAME="frame1">
<FRAME SRC="frame2.html" NAME="frame2">
</FRAMESET>

Part IX

Cool Things You Can Do with JavaScript

Everything you ever wanted to know about how to use JavaScript in your Web pages (but were afraid to ask!) is in this part. Some of the coding tips are HTML-based; others are pure JavaScript. Most of these examples show things you'll want to try out in your own Web pages; *all* of the examples come complete with working example code.

In this part . . .

- ✔ Adding multimedia to your Web page

- ✔ Integrating other components with JavaScript

- ✔ Hiding your JavaScript source code from prying eyes

- ✔ Validating user input and communicating the results to your users

Adding Multimedia to Your Web Page

You can add images, all kinds of different colors, sounds, and even animation to your Web pages.

Color

Using color is a good way to add interest and *flash* to your Web pages. You can specify different colors for any or all the items described in the following table. (*See also* Appendix B for a list of all of the predefined colors that you can use.)

HTML <BODY> Attribute	Description	JavaScript Syntax
BGCOLOR	Background color	document.bgColor
TEXT	Foreground color	document.fgColor
LINK	Unfollowed link color	document.linkColor
ALINK	Activated link color	document.alinkColor
VLINK	Followed link color	document.vlinkColor

Two ways exist to change the color of the elements in the preceding table: via HTML statements inside the body section of your HTML file, and via JavaScript statements. Here's an example of each approach:

```
<BODY BGCOLOR="lime"
TEXT="darkblue"
LINK="black"
ALINK="antiquewhite"
VLINK="orange">
```

```
document.fgColor = "yellow"
```

But wait! There's more. Here's one more way to change the color of text displayed in your Web page: the `fontcolor()` method of the `String` object. Here's how it works:

Syntax:

```
aString.fontcolor("someColor")
```

Example:

```
document.write("This is dark
    orchid.".fontcolor("darkorchid"))
```

Moving images

You can take three basic approaches to integrate animation and movies into your Web pages:

✦ **Create a hypertext link to an animation file:** Some popular animation file formats include .avi, .dvi, .fli, .mov, .mpg, and animated .gif. *See also* "Web-Surfing: Creating Hypertext Links" later in this part for the scoop on how to set up a hypertext link.

✦ **Add a plug-in that plays animation files:** One such plug-in is Shockwave for Director from Macromedia, which enables you to play Director movies inside your Web pages. *See also* "Calling Other Components from JavaScript" later in this part.

To learn more about the Shockwave for Director plug-in, visit the following URL:

```
http://www.macromedia.com/shockwave/
```

✦ **Use a Java applet that plays animation files:** To find out how to integrate your script with a Java applet, *see also* "Calling Other Components from JavaScript," later in this part.

Pictures

Inserting pictures into your Web page is brought to you courtesy of the HTML <IMG> tag. Here's an example:

```
<IMG SRC="images/mouse.gif" ALIGN="TOP"
ALT="[Rupert the Mouse]">
```

If you don't specify a path name for your image source (such as http://www.bogus.com/images/filename.gif), your Web browser looks for the image file in the directory where your .html file is located.

Sound

Adding sounds to your Web page can be a great attention-getter, but there's a downside. Sound files (which typically have extensions of .ra, .sbi, .snd, .au, or .wav) are notoriously huge, which means that users loading your sound-enabled Web page may have a long wait ahead of them. Remember, too, that not everyone on the Web is equipped with sound-playing software and speakers.

The best way to add sound to your Web page is to specify a link to a sound file. That way, users who know they aren't set up for sound (or who are in a hurry) can choose to skip your aural tidbit. *See also* "Web-Surfing: Creating Hypertext Links" later in this part to get all the details on creating links.

Calling Other Components from JavaScript

You can tie software components together with JavaScript to create knockout Web applications. At the time of this writing, you have three choices, depending on which Web browser you want to use to view your finished product: ActiveX components, Java applets, and Netscape plug-ins.

ActiveX components

ActiveX components are software modules that are compatible not only with Internet Explorer, but with non-Internet-related Microsoft client applications, too. The following code snippet shows how you can integrate an ActiveX component into a JavaScript script in Internet Explorer by using the <OBJECT> tag:

```
function showProperties() {
    alert("Label properties: "
        + document.myForm.sprlbl1.Angle + ", " +
        + document.myForm.sprlbl1.Alignment + ", " +
        + document.myForm.sprlbl1.BackStyle + ", " +
        + document.myForm.sprlbl1.Caption + ", " +
        + document.myForm.sprlbl1.FontName + ", " +
        + document.myForm.sprlbl1.FontSize)
}

</SCRIPT>
<BODY>
<FORM NAME="myForm">
<OBJECT
    classid="clsid:99B42120-6EC7-11CF-A6C7-
        00AA00A47DD2"
    id=sprlbl1
    width=150
    height=500
    vspace=0
    align=left>
    <param name="Angle" value="270">
    <param name="Alignment" value="2">
    <param name="BackStyle" value="0">
    <param name="Caption" value="JavaScript!">
    <param name="FontName" value="Times New Roman">
    <param name="FontSize" value="40">
    </OBJECT>
<INPUT TYPE="button" value="Look at control's
    properties"
NAME="showButton" onClick="showProperties()">
<BR><BR>
<INPUT TYPE="button" value="Call control's method"
    NAME="callButton"
onClick="document.myForm.sprlbl1.AboutBox()">
```

In the code above, the statements between the `<OBJECT>`...
`</OBJECT>` tags embed an ActiveX component in a Web page.
The showButton's onClick event handler calls a function
(showProperties()) that displays the embedded ActiveX
component's properties to the user, while the callButton's
onClick event handler calls a method (AboutBox()) on the
embedded component itself. *See also* the "ActiveX component"
section in Part I.

At the time of this writing, only the latest version of Internet
Explorer (3.01) can interact with ActiveX components, although a
plug-in for Navigator is being developed that may provide ActiveX
compatibility for Netscape Navigator.

Check out the following URL for a list of available ActiveX components, along with the unique programming information for each.
You'll need to hook 'em up to your JavaScript scripts (like their
class identifier, any parameters they require, and so forth):

```
http://www.microsoft.com/intdev/controls/
    ctrlref-f.htm
```

For the latest details on the development of a plug-in that can make
ActiveX components compatible with Navigator, visit this site:

```
http://www.ncompasslabs.com/products/
    scriptactive.htm
```

Java applets

You can embed Java applets into your Web pages with the help of
the `<APPLET>`...`</APPLET>` tag pair. *See also* Part I.

HTML support for Java applets is provided both by Navigator and
Internet Explorer; however, JavaScript/applet interaction is
currently only supported by Navigator.

Following is an example of a JavaScript statement that invokes a
method called changeText() on a Java applet (check out the
onClick event handler):

```
<APPLET CODEBASE="http://home.netscape.com/comprod/
    products/navigator/version_3.0/developer"
NAME="NervousApplet" CODE="NervousText.class"
    WIDTH=400 HEIGHT=50>
<PARAM NAME=text VALUE="Enter your text here.">
</APPLET>
<BR>
<INPUT NAME="InputText" TYPE=text SIZE=35
    VALUE="Enter your text here.">
<BR>
<INPUT TYPE=button WIDTH=200 VALUE="Click here to
    change text."
onClick="document.applets[0].changeText(form.InputText.value)">
```

To find out the names of applet properties and methods that you can access, you can either scout out other Web pages that embed the applet, or go right to the source (the applet developer) to get official documentation.

Netscape plug-ins

At the time of this writing, only Navigator's implementation of JavaScript can interact with plug-ins.

Netscape plug-ins are embedded into HTML files with the <EMBED> tag. *See also* the "Plug-in" section in Part I.

Before you try this example, you need to download the Envoy document management plug-in from Tumbleweed Software and install it in Navigator's /Program/plugins directory on your hard drive. Here's where you can find the Envoy plug-in:

```
http://www.tumbleweed.com/download.htm
```

The following code shows how to access an embedded Netscape plug-in's innards via JavaScript:

```
<HTML><HEAD><TITLE>Embedded Plug-In Example</TITLE>
<SCRIPT LANGUAGE="JavaScript">

function displayFlag(flagToDisplay) {
    document.envoyPlugin.setCurrentPage(flagToDisplay)
    document.envoyPlugin.executeCommand(601)
}

</SCRIPT>
</HEAD>
<BODY>
<FORM NAME="myForm">

<EMBED NAME="envoyPlugin"
SRC="http://www.tumbleweed.com/evy/flags.evy"
    WIDTH=300
HEIGHT=250
BORDER=0 INTERFACE=STATIC ZOOM=fitwidth
PLUGINSPAGE="http://www.tumbleweed.com/plugin.htm">

<H2> Select a flag to display:</H2>
<INPUT TYPE="radio" NAME="flagToDisplay"
onClick="displayFlag(1)"> U.S.
<INPUT TYPE="radio" NAME="flagToDisplay"
onClick="displayFlag(4)"> Germany
<INPUT TYPE="radio" NAME="flagToDisplay"
onClick="displayFlag(8)"> Canada

<INPUT TYPE="button" NAME="test"
VALUE="Get Number of Embeds"
onClick="alert('Number of embedded plug-ins in this
    document: '
+ embeds.length)"
```

```
</FORM>
</BODY>
</HTML>
```

The plug-in is embedded in the page with the `<EMBED>` tag. When a user selects one of the radio buttons defined in the form (the choices are U.S., Germany, or Canada), the `displayFlag()` function is called. The values that are being passed into the `displayFlag()` function (1, 4, and 8) mean something special to the plug-in. To get hold of plug-in specific values and methods, you can either scout out other scripts that access the plug-in, or go right to the source (the plug-in developer) to get official plug-in documentation. For instance, you wouldn't know that the Envoy plug-in supported the methods being called from `displayFlag()` —`setCurrentPage()` and `executeCommand()` (or how to call them) unless the plug-in developer clued you in.

Creating Your Own JavaScript Objects

As you may know, true object-oriented languages allow you to inherit from existing objects to create your own new objects (that is, base new objects on old ones so you can get away with writing less code). Because JavaScript isn't technically object-oriented (it's object-based), you can't inherit from existing objects to create your own objects in JavaScript, but you *can* make your own objects from scratch using the new operator and a function or two. In the code example that follows, I create a virtual pet that can talk. Read on for all the exciting details.

```
function talkFunction(kindOfPet){
    if (kindOfPet == "dog") {
        document.writeln("bow-wow!")
    }
    else {
        if (kindOfPet == "cat") {
            document.writeln("meow-meow-meow")
        }
    }
    else {
        document.writeln("I'm speechless.")
    }
}
function Pet(inputName, inputKind, inputColor) {
    this.name = inputName
    this.kind = inputKind
    this.color = inputColor
    this.speak = talkFunction(inputKind)
}
```

Given the two functions shown in the preceding example, you can create as many instances of Pet as you want:

```
var myCat = new Pet("Boots", "cat", "orange
    striped")
var myDog = new Pet("King", "dog", "gray and
    brown")
var myFish = new Pet("Bubbles", "goldfish", "or-
    ange")
```

And when you want one of your virtual pets to speak, all you have to do is this:

```
myCat.speak
myDog.speak
myFish.speak
```

Because myCat, myDog, and myFish contain both properties and methods (okay, *one* method), they're bona fide, card-carrying objects. They can even contain or be contained by other objects. For example, you may want to create an object called Person and show a relationship between your instances of Person and Pet, like this:

```
function Person(inputName, inputAge, inputSex,
    inputPet){
    this.name = inputName
    this.age = inputAge
    this.sex = inputSex
    this.pet = inputPet
}
```

```
var aDog = new Pet("King", "dog", "gray and brown")
```

```
var petOwner = new Person("Bertha", "33", "Female",
    aDog)
alert("Here is Bertha's dog's name: " +
petOwner.pet.name)
```

Take a look at the last three JavaScript statements in the code snippet above. See how an instance of Pet is being created and named aDog? Directly after that, a new Person, called petOwner, is created — and aDog (the entire object) is being passed to the Person constructor. To prove that this association worked properly, the last statement displays the value for petOwner.pet.name — which (and you can try this out for yourself) is "King."

Displaying Scrolling Text

The following example displays scrolling text in the browser's status line, but you could display it anywhere else on the Web page just as easily.

```
function displayBanner() {
    var lengthToScroll
    var message = "Your message here..."
    var rateToScroll = 85
    var displayLength = 100

    // increasing rateToScroll slows down the
    scroll
    lengthToScroll = (rateToScroll/message.length)
    + 1
    for(var i=0; i<=lengthToScroll; i++) {
        message += " " + message
    }

    // place it in the status bar
    status = message.substring(position, position +
        displayLength)

    // set new position
    if(position++ == message.length){
        position = 0
    }

    // repeat scrolling action
    id = setTimeout("displayBanner()",1000/35)
}
</SCRIPT>
...
<BODY onLoad="window.status=displayBanner(); return
    true"
onUnload="window.status=''">
```

As soon as the Web page is loaded, the onLoad event handler in the code above calls displayBanner(), which stuffs the message "Your message here..." in the status line. After a brief pause, displayBanner() calls *itself* — this time shifting the position of the displayed message slightly. For as long as the page is loaded, displayBanner() keeps calling itself every so often, shifting the message position each time so that it appears to the user as though the message is scrolling.

Use scrolling text sparingly — it can be a good way to draw attention to something on your page, but misused, it can be very annoying! Not only do many users find it distracting, but rumors are going around that over time, scrolling schemes like the preceding one can cause a user's browser to slow or crash (depending, of course, on the version of the browser the user has installed).

Displaying the Contents of Nested Objects

A *nested* object is one that is contained inside another object. For example: a document contains a form (which is why you have to refer to it as document.form), so the form is considered to be a nested object (it's *nested* inside a document).

You can create your own nested objects. But what if you nest
objects a couple of levels deep? For debugging, you'll probably
want to be able to take a look at the contents of an entire object,
including the contents of all the objects it contains (and all the
objects each of *them* contains, and so on). The following listing
contains some example code that shows you how to inspect the
contents of nested objects.

```
var displayString = ""
function buildDisplay(inputObject,
    inputObjectName){
    // These two lines set typeOfObject to the text
    // representation of inputObject
    var typeOfObject = ""
    typeOfObject += inputObject

    if (typeOfObject.substring(1,7) != "object") {
        // the object is a plain old field
        displayString += "\n" + inputObject + "="
                        + inputObjectName + "\n"
    }

    else {
        // the object contains other objects
        displayString += "Displaying object " +
    inputObject
    + "\n"

        for (var eachProperty in inputObject) {
            var nestedObjectName = ""
            nestedObjectName += inputObject[eachProperty]
            var nestedObject = inputObject[eachProperty]

            displayString += eachProperty + "=" +
            nestedObjectName + "\n"

            if (nestedObjectName.substring(1,7) ==
    "object") {
                // the object contains still MORE objects
                // so call this method again (this is
    called
                // "recursion")
                buildDisplay(nestedObject,
    nestedObjectName)
            }
        }
    }
}
```

How does this code snippet work? Well, assume that you call
buildDisplay() with an object called recipeBook, which is filled
with three recipes. Each recipe, in turn, contains a name and a list
of ingredients. The buildDisplay() function in the preceding
example walks through the nested objects and displays the field
values each contains, like this:

```
Displaying object recipeBook
     Displaying object recipe
name = chocolate cake
Displaying object listOfIngredients
     ingredientOne = flour
     ingredientTwo = sugar
     ingredientThree = eggs
     ingredientFour = cocoa
Displaying object recipe
name = white cake
Displaying object listOfIngredients
     ingredientOne = flour
     ingredientTwo = sugar
     ingredientThree = eggs
     ingredientFour = vanilla
Displaying object recipe
name = rum cake
Displaying object listOfIngredients
     ingredientOne = flour
     ingredientTwo = sugar
     ingredientThree = eggs
     ingredientFour = rum extract
```

Formatting Money Fields

It's entirely possible that you may want your Web pages to display money values, and nothing looks tackier than displaying a money value as "123.44444400" (which is what JavaScript does when it's left to its own devices). Fortunately, you have a choice — you can use the functions in the following code listing to validate and format any input field you want to constrain to money values.

```
function scrubData(inputValue) {

    // This function deletes digits that aren't
    numbers
    // or periods.  If a non-money-based digit is
    // encountered (something other than a "$", a
    ".",
    // or a space) an error is displayed.

    var returnValue = ""
    for (var i=0; i<inputValue.length; i++) {
      var digit = inputValue.charAt(i)
      if (parseFloat(digit) || digit == "."
                            || digit == "0") {
        // digit is a number or period, so keep it
        returnValue += digit
      }
      else {
        if (digit != " " && digit != "$" && digit !=
    ".") {
          // something weird encountered
```

(continued)

(continued)

```
        alert("Please enter a non-zero numeric
  value.")
        break
      }
    }
  }
  return returnValue
}

function asMoney(inputValue) {
  // First, make sure that input value is "clean"
  var scrubValue = scrubData(inputValue)

  // Declare some temporary variables
  var returnString = ""
  var tempNumber = 0
  var tempString = ""
  tempNumber = Math.round(scrubValue * 100)

  // Manipulate the number so we know what we're
  // dealing with
  if (tempNumber < 10) {
    tempString = "00" + tempNumber
  }
  else if (tempNumber < 100) {
    tempString = "0" + tempNumber
  }
  else {
    tempString = "" + tempNumber
  }

  if (tempString.length > 9) {
    alert("Sorry, can't process numbers > one
  million.")
    return scrubValue
  }

  // This next section builds the return string
  // by starting with a dollar sign, then breaking
   up the
  // number into sections, then placing commas and
  // periods between the sections as appropriate.

  returnString = "$"

  if (tempString.length > 5) {
    // Need to add at least one comma
    if (tempString.length == 6) {
      returnString += tempString.substring(0,1) +
  "," +
        tempString.substring(1,tempString.length-2)
    }
    else if (tempString.length == 7) {
      returnString += tempString.substring(0,2) +
  "," +
        tempString.substring(2,tempString.length-2)
    }
```

```
else if (tempString.length == 8) {
  returnString += tempString.substring(0,3) +
"," +
    tempString.substring(3,tempString.length-2)
}
else if (tempString.length == 9) {
  // Need to add two commas
  returnString += tempString.substring(0,1) +
"," +
    tempString.substring(1,4) + "," +
    tempString.substring(4,tempString.length-2)
}
}
else { // No commas necessary
  returnString = "$" +
    tempString.substring(0,(tempString.length-2))
}
// add in the cents
  returnString += "." +
    tempString.substring((tempString.length -
    2),tempString.length)

// Return the newly formatted string back
// to the caller
return returnString
}
...
Enter a number and click anywhere else on the page.
  You can also use the following symbols if you
  want: $ , .
<INPUT TYPE="text" NAME="desiredSalary" SIZE=15
onBlur="document.myForm.desiredSalary.value =
  asMoney(this.value)">
```

Here's what happens in the code above when a user types a
number (say, 66666) into the desiredSalary field and then clicks
elsewhere, thus blurring the field:

- ✦ asMoney() first calls scrubValue() to remove any spaces,
  dollar signs, commas, or periods typed in (if a user has typed
  in some character values, an error is displayed on-screen).

- ✦ asMoney() then adds in money punctuation by counting
  backwards. Two spaces back and it adds a decimal point;
  three spaces back and it adds a comma; finally, it tacks a
  dollar sign on the front.

- ✦ onBlur assigns the desiredSalary field the newly format-
  ted value.

The result? Instead of the 66666 originally typed into the field, the
value of the field post-event handler will be $666.66.

Getting Started with a Bare-Bones HTML Template

For a jump-start on your very first JavaScript-enabled Web page, try this template.

```
<HTML>
<HEAD><TITLE>Your Title Goes Here</TITLE>

<SCRIPT LANGUAGE="JavaScript">
<!--
// Put your JavaScript statements here
// -->
</SCRIPT>

</HEAD>

<BODY>
<FORM NAME="myForm">
<!- This is an HTML comment.  You can use this
commenting convention anywhere in your HTML file
except between a set of SCRIPT tags. And by the
    way,
don't put angle brackets inside these comments if
    you
can help it — doing so confuses the HTML inter-
    preter.
->
</FORM>
</BODY>

</HTML>
```

Hiding JavaScript Source Code from Users

Two different scenarios exist when hiding your JavaScript source code which might make sense. One scenario is hiding your source from users running JavaScript-enabled Web browsers. At present, it's rare that folks hide their source code from each other using this mechanism. After all, as you probably know, the legacy of the Internet is a spirit of sharing and open exchange. Still, if you want to do it, you can do so by following the example in the following section.

The second scenario, hiding your JavaScript source from users running browsers that can't interpret your scripting code anyway, is *always* a good idea.

From JavaScript-enabled browsers

When you create a JavaScript-enabled Web page and install it on a Web server, folks all across the world can get access to your HTML/JavaScript source. How? The same way *you* get access to *their* source code — by choosing View⇨Document Source (in Netscape Navigator) or View⇨Source (in Internet Explorer).

If you want to nip this kind of information-sharing, tree-hugging free-for-all in the bud, separate your JavaScript statements from the rest of your HTML statements and put them in a separate file with a .js filename extension. Then, in the <SCRIPT>... </SCRIPT> tag pair, specify the name of the source file, like this:

```
<SCRIPT LANGUAGE="JavaScript"
SRC="http://www.mydomain.com/myscript.js">
</SCRIPT>
```

Besides hiding your JavaScript source from prying eyes, bundling related JavaScript functions into one file makes it easier for you to reuse those functions in multiple Web pages. Instead of having to copy the function definitions into every HTML file in which you want to use the functions, all you have to do is reference the .js file in your Web pages, as shown above!

If you want to test this code with a file on your local machine, you can. Just set the SRC attribute equal to the name of your JavaScript file (for example, SRC="mySwellFunctions.js") and put that file in the same directory as your HTML file.

At the time of this writing, the SRC attribute is supported only by Navigator 3.0.

From non-JavaScript-enabled browsers

Users with non-JavaScript-enabled browsers who attempt to load your JavaScript-enabled Web page will be subjected to a frightfully ugly display: your JavaScript source code! (Since their browsers can't interpret JavaScript source code, the browsers assume it's text that's meant to be presented on-screen.) To keep this from happening (without affecting users running Navigator or Internet Explorer), all you have to do is add special comment characters just below the beginning <SCRIPT> tag and just above the ending <SCRIPT> tag, like so:

```
<SCRIPT LANGUAGE="JavaScript">
<!--
function someFunction() {
    ...
}
```

(continued)

(continued)

```
function someOtherFunction() {
    ...
}
// -->
</SCRIPT>
```

As you can see in the preceding code snippet, the comments must be placed just inside the `<SCRIPT>...</SCRIPT>` tags. Also, note that these are special comments; they're neither standard HTML (which look like this: `<!-    ->`) nor standard JavaScript comments (which look like this: `//`).

Interacting with Cookies

A *cookie* is a chunk of browser-related (technically, client-related) information that a program on a Web server can store on the client machine. Once a cookie has been stored on a client, the next time the same server and client communicate, the server can take a look at the stored cookie and make some decisions based on it — for example, what to display to a client user and how best to display it.

The following example gives you a taste of the kind of application that cookies can help you build. It's the Netscape PowerStart application, an application that enables users to create their own custom Web pages. PowerStart uses a JavaScript-enabled Web page, which displays a menu that offers all kinds of choices regarding Web-page color, graphics, layout, and content. Users decide which of these features they want, and when they are finished making their decisions, they click on the Build button, which saves their preferences on their machines.

After that, each time that a user selects the `MyPage` URL from the Netscape home page, the locally stored preferences in the file cookies.txt are extracted and used to dynamically create a custom Web page. Check out the following code listing (borrowed from the Netscape PowerStart Web page) to get a peek at how cookie-JavaScript interaction is handled:

```
function SetCookie (name, thevalue) {
    ...
    // what could be simpler?
    document.cookie = name + ' = ' + thevalue + ';
    ...
}

...
```

```
function resetall () {
    var warning = 'Sure you want to start over?
    You' +
        br() + 'will lose all of your custom set-
    tings.'
    ...
    if (confirm(warning)) {
        ...
        parent.SetCookie('p1', 'blank')
        parent.SetCookie('note', 'Reminder: Add
    this page to your bookmarks list.')
    }
    ...
}
...
<INPUT TYPE="button" NAME="reset" VALUE=" Start
    Over " onClick="resetall();">
</HTML>
```

When a user loads the PowerStart page, customizes her home page, and then clicks the Start Over button on the left-hand frame, `resetall()` is called. The statements inside `resetAll()` call `SetCookie()` to "blank out" the data stored in the cookie, so the user can start again fresh.

To confirm that these things are really taking place, I encourage you to load PowerStart at URL `http://personal.netscape.com /custom/modify.html` and scroll to the very bottom of the left-hand frame, where you'll see the "Start Over" button. Customize your personal Web page first, then click on Start Over and see what happens!

At the time of this writing, client-side cookie support isn't provided in Internet Explorer 3.0.

Loading and Running a JavaScript Script

To load and run JavaScript scripts, all you have to do is load a Web page that contains embedded JavaScript statements. When you interact with the loaded page (click on a button, type in some text, that kind of thing), your browser's built-in JavaScript interpreter recognizes the JavaScript statements and performs them for you automatically. Currently, only Netscape Navigator and Microsoft Internet Explorer support JavaScript.

There's a slight difference between loading a JavaScript-enabled Web page that's on your local machine and one that's on a Web server.

	Navigator	*Internet Explorer*
To load a file from your machine:	File⇨Open File	File⇨Open
To load a file from a Web server:	File⇨Open Location	File⇨Open

Looking at JavaScript Source Code

One of the best things about learning JavaScript is that when you see a really cool script, you can immediately take a behind-the-scenes look at the JavaScript and HTML code responsible. Here's how:

+ If you're running Navigator and have loaded an interesting Web page, choose View⇨Document Source. If the page contains multiple frames, you can also click on a particular frame and select View⇨Frame Source to see just the code for that frame.

+ If you're running Internet Explorer, choose View⇨Source to see a Web page's source code.

Making an Embedded Image Respond to User Events

Ever wondered how folks created those really cool clickable maps? Well, here's the secret!

```
<MAP NAME="thistleMap">

<AREA NAME="leftHalf" COORDS="0,0,150,300"
    HREF="javascript:displayMessage()"
onMouseOver="self.status='Left side of the pic-
    ture'; return true"
onMouseOut="self.status=''; return true">

<AREA NAME="rightHalf" COORDS="0,0,600,600"
HREF="javascript:displayMessage2()"
onMouseOver="self.status='Right side of the pic-
    ture'; return true"
onMouseOut="self.status=''; return true">

</MAP>

<IMG NAME="currentImage"
SRC="images/thistle.gif" ALIGN="MIDDLE"
    ALT="[Scottish thistles]"
USEMAP="#thistleMap">
```

This code snippet produces an image that displays the text "Right side of the picture" in the status line when the user moves the mouse over the right half of the image, and displays the text "Left side of the picture" when the user (you guessed it) moves the mouse over the left half of the image.

At the time of this writing, this approach works best in Navigator 3.0. (The preceding code, interpreted by Internet Explorer 3.0, displays Shortcut to javascript:displayMessage in the status bar when a user moves a mouse over the left half of the image.)

Making Your Script Compatible with Non-JavaScript-Enabled Browsers

The quickest, lowest-common-denominator way to make your scripts presentable to non-JavaScript-enabled browsers is to follow the example in the section "Hiding JavaScript Source Code from Users" earlier in this part. The approach you'll find there ensures that browsers that can't interpret your JavaScript source code at least won't assume the source code is text and splash it all over the page for the user to see.

A more comprehensive solution is to use navigator properties to determine what brand and version of browser a user is using to load your Web page right away, before you display anything. After you know what you're dealing with, you can create two different HTML files and present the appropriate version for each kind of browser — JavaScript-friendly and non-JavaScript-friendly. More work? Absolutely. Is it worth it? It may be, if you want to dazzle the sizable portion of the global Web audience that for some reason or other hasn't yet gotten around to upgrading to a JavaScript-enabled Web browser!

```
if !(navigator.appName == "Netscape" &&
    navigator.appVersion.substring(0,1) == 3) {
    // The user isn't running Netscape Navigator 3.x
    // so they might not be able to see the fancy
    // stuff. If you want, you can automatically
    load
    // a plain-vanilla version of your Web page for
    them.
}
```

Providing Feedback to Users with Pop-Up Messages

Pop-up messages are a great way to call a user's attention to something (like, they entered the wrong value for a field). Generally, you'll want to assign one of these messages to the event handler of some input element — a button's onClick event handler, for example. Be aware, though, that pop-up messages are fairly intrusive; users have to stop everything and deal with them before they can continue with what they were doing.

JavaScript contains three different kinds of pop-up messages, which you can create using three different window methods: alert(), confirm(), and prompt().

Method	Tells the User...	Input Parameter(s)	Return Value
alert()	Hey! Something just happened!	string to display	none
confirm()	Yes or no? Answer me!	string to display	true (OK) false (Cancel)
prompt()	You need to enter a value.	string to display	user-entered value, if any; else null default value to display (optional)

Following are examples for each method.

```
alert("Please enter your phone number in the
    following format: (123) 456-7890")

var answer = confirm("Do you really want to order
    5,000 toenail clippers?")

var numberOfOrders = prompt("Enter the number of
    orders you want to place", 1)
```

Saving JavaScript Files

When you find a really inspirational JavaScript-enabled Web page, chances are that you may want to save it so that you can study it, print it out, frame it, or maybe even (gasp!) borrow portions of it for your own Web page. You've got a choice of two formats when you save JavaScript-enabled HTML files:

+ HTML source code

+ WYSIWYG (what you see is what you get, or plain old text)

Saving JavaScript files as HTML source code

+ If you're running Navigator 3.0, you can save HTML source by choosing File⇨Save As⇨Save as type⇨HTML Files.

+ In Internet Explorer, it's almost the same: choose File⇨Save As File⇨Save as type⇨HTML (*.htm, *.html).

Whichever browser you're running, just be sure that the file name you create ends with .html or .htm.

Saving JavaScript files as text

+ If you're running Navigator 3.0, you can save the text of a Web page by choosing File⇨Save As⇨Save as type⇨Plain Text (*.txt).

+ In Internet Explorer, it's almost the same: choose File⇨Save As File⇨Save as type⇨Plain Text (*.txt).

Choose a file name that ends with .txt, and you're home free.

Using JavaScript to Calculate Values for HTML Tags

Navigator 3.0 gives you the ability to calculate values using JavaScript statements and then assign these calculated values to HTML tag attributes. The following sample code affects the `<BODY>...</BODY>` tag pair, but you can assign a calculated value to any HTML attribute.

```
function getRandomColor() {
    var today = new Date()
    var x = today.getSeconds()
    if (x < 5) { return "maroon" }
    else if (x > 5 && x < 10) { return "yellow" }
    else if (x > 10 && x < 15) { return "green" }
    else if (x > 15 && x < 20) { return
"antiquewhite" }
    else if (x > 20 && x < 25) { return "azure" }
    else if (x > 25 && x < 30) { return "chocolate" }
    else if (x > 35 && x < 40) { return "red" }
    else if (x > 40 && x < 45) { return "lavender" }
    else if (x > 45 && x < 50) { return
"cornflowerblue"}
    else if (x > 50 && x > 55) { return "beige"}
}
</SCRIPT>
</HEAD>
<BODY BGCOLOR="&{getRandomColor()};">
```

Each time you load a Web page that contains the preceding example code, you see a different background color. What fun!

Remember: When you assign a JavaScript statement to an HTML attribute, you need to remember to surround the JavaScript statement with an ampersand and opening curly brace (`&{`) in front and a closing curly brace and a semicolon (`};`) bringing up the rear.

Validating User Input

You can take two different approaches to validate the input your users type into your HTML form. One approach is to take a look at the entire form input in one fell swoop, right before you submit it to a CGI program. Another approach is to examine each input field as soon as the user finishes with it (to see immediately if it's up to snuff). These approaches aren't mutually exclusive — in fact, you probably want to use both.

Validating before the form is submitted

The onSubmit event handler of the form object is a good place to
do what is called *consistency editing,* which is validating that the
input a user types in is valid (taken as a whole). For example, a
user may specify himself as "Single" in one field *and* enter a value
for "Spouse's name" in another field. Clearly, both values can't be
correct, because they contradict each other. It's this type of
inconsistency between values that you can check right before you
pack up your form data and ship it off to a CGI program.

```
function doesExist(inputValue) {
    var aCharExists=0
    if (inputValue) {
        for (var i=0; i<inputValue.length; i++) {
            if (inputValue.charAt(i) != " ") {
                aCharExists = 1
            }
        }
    }
    if (!aCharExists) {
        return 0
    }
    else {
        return 1
    }
}

function editFormForConsistency() {
    if ((document.myForm.single.value == "Y" &&
        doesExist
    (document.myForm.spouseName.value))
        ||
        (document.myForm.single.value == "N" &&
        !doesExist(document.myForm.spouseName.value)))
    {
                return false
    }
    else {
        return true
    }
}
...
<FORM NAME="myForm"
onSubmit="return editFormForConsistency()">

<BR>Are you single? (Y or N)
<INPUT TYPE="text" NAME="single" VALUE="Y" SIZE=1>
<BR>Name of spouse: <INPUT TYPE="text"
    NAME="spouseName">
<BR><BR><BR><INPUT TYPE="submit" VALUE="Submit!">
```

Validating one field at a time

Validating one field at a time is sometimes called *field-level validation,* and it's the quickest way to give users feedback on their input. This section contains examples of the most common field-level validation criteria.

Existence:

One way to make sure that a user fills in a field is to examine the value of the field as soon as the user finishes with it to make sure that a value exists. Here's how:

```
function doesExist(inputValue, inputExpected) {
    var aCharExists=0
    if (inputValue) {
        for (var i=0; i<inputValue.length; i++) {
            if (inputValue.charAt(i) != " ") {
                aCharExists = 1
            }
        }
    }
    if (!aCharExists) {
        alert("Please enter a " + inputExpected)
    }
}
...
<BR>Company name:
<INPUT TYPE="text" NAME="companyName" VALUE=""
    SIZE=35
onBlur="doesExist(this.value, 'company name')">
```

When a user clicks on the text field called companyName and then clicks somewhere else on the page, this code snippet springs into action. First, it determines whether the input value exists at all. If it does, the code loops through the input value, one character at a time, to make sure that something other than all spaces were entered. (Technically, a bunch of spaces in a row is an "existing" value to JavaScript; humans, however, generally have other ideas!) If no nonspace characters were typed in, this function triggers a pop-up message to alert the user.

Numeric:

Sometimes, you may want to make sure that a user supplies a numeric value for a field (an age field, perhaps, or a price field). Depending on your needs, the JavaScript functions parseInt, parseFloat, and isNaN (all of which are discussed at length in Part V) may be just what the doctor ordered.

These functions, however, return the computer equivalent of a thumbs-up if the first digit is numeric, regardless of what the user types in after that. So, if a user types in **8abcd**, parseInt, parseFloat, and isNaN would give that value their blessing! If you want to do a more thorough validation job, try the function listed in the following example.

```
function isANumber(inputValue){
    if (!parseFloat(inputValue)) {
        alert("Please enter a numeric value.")
    }
    else {
        for (var i=0; i<inputValue.length; i++) {
            if (inputValue.charAt(i) != " ") {
                if(!parseFloat(inputValue.charAt(i)))
            {
                    alert("Please enter a numeric
value.")
                    break
                }
            }
        }
    }
}
...
Number of items you wish to purchase:
<INPUT TYPE="text" NAME="numberItems" VALUE=""
    SIZE=5
onBlur="isANumber(this.value)">
```

These JavaScript statements, repeated from the isANumber() function in the code snippet above, cause isANumber() to ignore any blank spaces that the user may accidentally type next to a number. That keeps an error from popping up if a user types in a space.

```
if (inputValue.charAt(i) != " ") {
    // if we got here, the character's not a space
    if (!parseFloat(inputValue.charAt(i))) {
        alert("Please enter a numeric value.")
        break
    }
}
```

Conforming to a pattern:

All e-mail addresses follow a common pattern, and it's conceivable that you may want to make sure that the address that your user enters into an e-mail address field is valid. (After all, you may be relying on the address to send information, an invoice, or what have you.) Other examples of numbers that have common patterns are phone numbers, social security numbers, and account numbers. Here's how you can go about validating a phone number input field (you can adapt the code to validate any pattern you want):

```
function isAPhoneNumber(inputValue){
    if (inputValue) {
        var openParen = inputValue.substring(0,1)
        var areaCode = inputValue.substring(1,4)
        var closeParen = inputValue.substring(4,5)
        var exchange = inputValue.substring(5,8)
        var dash = inputValue.substring(8,9)
        var line = inputValue.substring(9,13)

        if (
            (openParen != "(")          ||
            (!isANumber(areaCode))      ||
            (closeParen != ")")         ||
            (!isANumber(exchange))      ||
            (dash != "-")               ||
            (!isANumber(line))){
                alert("Please enter phone number in
the following format: (123)456-7890")
            }
        }
}
...
<BR>Please enter your home phone number
<BR>in the following format: (123)456-7890
<INPUT TYPE="text" NAME="homePhone" VALUE=""
    SIZE=13
onBlur="isAPhoneNumber(this.value)">
```

You may notice the use of a function called isANumber() in the
preceding example. It's the same isANumber() that was designed
in a preceding section to validate numeric fields! Here it does
double-duty, validating the numeric portions of a phone number.
Ah, sweet reuse.

Web-Surfing: Creating Hypertext Links

Hypertext links are what the Web's all about. This section shows
you how you can use them effectively.

Creating links between Web pages

Linking two Web pages is pretty easy. All you have to do is define a
link with the <A>...</A> tag, as shown below. (**See also**
"Hypertext link" in Part I.)

```
<A HREF="http://www.netscape.com"> Netscape's home
    page
```

If you're linking to a specific place on another Web page, called an
anchor, your statement would look more like this:

```
<A HREF="http://www.netscape.com#someAnchor"> A
    certain place on Netscape's home page
```

To see what anchors are available on other people's Web pages, view their HTML source code. To see how to view source code, **see also** "Looking at JavaScript Source Code," earlier in this part.

Creating links within a single Web page

In order to link from one part of a page to another, you need to define an anchor. An *anchor* is a piece of text that some other piece of text (a *link*) can link *to*. Here's an example:

```
<H1><CENTER>How to Stay Fit in Your 100's
   </CENTER></H1>
<A NAME="TOC"><H2>Table of Contents</H2></A>
<P>

<A HREF="#CHAP1">Chapter 1.</A><BR>
<A HREF="#CHAP2">Chapter 2.</A><BR>
<A HREF="#CHAP3">Chapter 3.</A><BR>

<A NAME="CHAP1"><H3>Chapter 1: Aerobic Fitness
   </H3></A>
<P>Chapter 1 text would go here, and it might be
several paragraphs (even pages) long.
<BR>

<A NAME="CHAP2"><H3>Chapter 2:  Eating Well</H3>
   </A>
<P>Chapter 2 text would go here.  Pretend that
this chapter is really long.  What if someone read
through Chapter 2 and then decided to read Chapter
   1?
Unless there was a link back to Chapter 1 (more
likely, a link back to the Table of Contents) it
would be hard for the user to scroll to the
correct starting point.
<BR><BR>
<A HREF="#TOC">Back to Table of Contents</A>
<P>

<A NAME="CHAP3"><H3>Chapter 3: Stress Reduction
   through Pet Ownership</H3></A>
<P>Chapter 3 text would go here.  When you're
designing multiple Web pages, consider putting a
button at the bottom of each page that lets the
user pop back to the first page (your <I>home</I>
   page).
<BR><BR>
<A HREF="#TOC">Back to Table of Contents</A>
```

Lots of anchors are being created in the preceding code example: TOC, CHAP1, CHAP2, and CHAP3. Notice how anchors are always referenced with a hash symbol (#) in front of them? The hash symbol must always be the first character of an anchor name. **See also** the "Hypertext anchor" section in Part I.

Reserved Words

Most of the keywords listed in this appendix mean something special to the JavaScript interpreter. The others are reserved for future incorporation; so even though some of these words aren't used for anything right now, you still get an error if you use any of the words in this list to name variables, functions, methods, or objects.

JavaScript reserved words

abstract	int
boolean	interface
break	long
byte	native
case	new
catch	null
char	package
class	private
const	protected
continue	public
default	return
do	short
double	static
else	super
extends	switch
false	synchronized
final	this
finally	throw
float	throws
for	transient
function	true
goto	try
if	var
implements	void
import	while
in	with
instanceof	

Color Values

Table B-1 contains an alphabetical listing of all of the predefined colors available to you in JavaScript. As you look through the list, remember that setting a form element's color to the string "aliceblue" is equivalent to setting it equal to the RGB triplet value "F0F8FF" — the choice of format is yours.

You can create your own custom colors by stringing together your very own red, green, and blue hexadecimal triplets. Here's how: In the hexadecimal scheme of things, the lowest two-digit number you can have is 00 (or 0 in decimal), the highest is FF (or 255 in decimal), and the progression for each digit looks like this:

```
0, 1, 2, 3, 4, 5, 6, 7, 8, 9, A, B, C, D,
   E, F
```

Start with a color from the list in Table B-1 that's close to what you want — for instance, *salmon*. If you're looking for something with a little more red in it, increase the red portion of the value (FA) to FB. If you're looking for a shade that's just a touch less blue, reduce the blue portion of the value (72) to, say, 66. You get the idea.

Table B-1		*Predefined Color Values*		
Color	*Red*	*Green*	*Blue*	*RGB Triplet*
aliceblue	F0	F8	FF	F0F8FF
antiquewhite	FA	EB	D7	FAEBD7
aqua	00	FF	FF	00FFFF
aquamarine	7F	FF	D4	7FFFD4
azure	F0	FF	FF	F0FFFF
beige	F5	F5	DC	F5F5DC
bisque	FF	E4	C4	FFE4C4
black	00	00	00	000000
blanchedalmond	FF	EB	CD	FFEBCD
blue	00	00	FF	0000FF
blueviolet	8A	2B	E2	8A2BE2
brown	A5	2A	2A	A52A2A
burlywood	DE	B8	87	DEB887
cadetblue	5F	9E	A0	5F9EA0
chartreuse	7F	FF	00	7FFF00
chocolate	D2	69	1E	D2691E
coral	FF	7F	50	FF7F50
cornflowerblue	64	95	ED	6495ED
cornsilk	FF	F8	DC	FFF8DC
crimson	DC	14	3C	DC143C
cyan	00	FF	FF	00FFFF
darkblue	00	00	8B	00008B
darkcyan	00	8B	8B	008B8B
darkgoldenrod	B8	86	0B	B8860B
darkgray	A9	A9	A9	A9A9A9
darkgreen	00	64	00	006400
darkkhaki	BD	B7	6B	BDB76B
darkmagenta	8B	00	8B	8B008B
darkolivegreen	55	6B	2F	556B2F
darkorange	FF	8C	00	FF8C00
darkorchid	99	32	CC	9932CC
darkred	8B	00	00	8B0000
darksalmon	E9	96	7A	E9967A
darkseagreen	8F	BC	8F	8FBC8F

Color	Red	Green	Blue	RGB Triplet
darkslateblue	48	3D	8B	483D8B
darkslategray	2F	4F	4F	2F4F4F
darkturquoise	00	CE	D1	00CED1
darkviolet	94	00	D3	9400D3
deeppink	FF	14	93	FF1493
deepskyblue	00	BF	FF	00BFFF
dimgray	69	69	69	696969
dodgerblue	1E	90	FF	1E90FF
firebrick	B2	22	22	B22222
floralwhite	FF	FA	F0	FFFAF0
forestgreen	22	8B	22	228B22
fuchsia	FF	00	FF	FF00FF
gainsboro	DC	DC	DC	DCDCDC
ghostwhite	F8	F8	FF	F8F8FF
gold	FF	D7	00	FFD700
goldenrod	DA	A5	20	DAA520
gray	80	80	80	808080
green	00	80	00	008000
greenyellow	AD	FF	2F	ADFF2F
honeydew	F0	FF	F0	F0FFF0
hotpink	FF	69	B4	FF69B4
indianred	CD	5C	5C	CD5C5C
indigo	4B	00	82	4B0082
ivory	FF	FF	F0	FFFFF0
khaki	F0	E6	8C	F0E68C
lavender	E6	E6	FA	E6E6FA
lavenderblush	FF	F0	F5	FFF0F5
lawngreen	7C	FC	00	7CFC00
lemonchiffon	FF	FA	CD	FFFACD
lightblue	AD	D8	E6	ADD8E6
lightcoral	F0	80	80	F08080
lightcyan	E0	FF	FF	E0FFFF
lightgoldenrodyellow	FA	FA	D2	FAFAD2
lightgreen	90	EE	90	90EE90
lightgrey	D3	D3	D3	D3D3D3

(continued)

Color	*Red*	*Green*	*Blue*	*RGB Triplet*
lightpink	FF	B6	C1	FFB6C1
lightsalmon	FF	A0	7A	FFA07A
lightseagreen	20	B2	AA	20B2AA
lightskyblue	87	CE	FA	87CEFA
lightslategray	77	88	99	778899
lightsteelblue	B0	C4	DE	B0C4DE
lightyellow	FF	FF	E0	FFFFE0
lime	00	FF	00	00FF00
limegreen	32	CD	32	32CD32
linen	FA	F0	E6	FAF0E6
magenta	FF	00	FF	FF00FF
maroon	80	00	00	800000
mediumaquamarine	66	CD	AA	66CDAA
mediumblue	00	00	CD	0000CD
mediumorchid	BA	55	D3	BA55D3
mediumpurple	93	70	DB	9370DB
mediumseagreen	3C	B3	71	3CB371
mediumslateblue	7B	68	EE	7B68EE
mediumspringgreen	00	FA	9A	00FA9A
mediumturquoise	48	D1	CC	48D1CC
mediumvioletred	C7	15	85	C71585
midnightblue	19	19	70	191970
mintcream	F5	FF	FA	F5FFFA
mistyrose	FF	E4	E1	FFE4E1
moccasin	FF	E4	B5	FFE4B5
navajowhite	FF	DE	AD	FFDEAD
navy	00	00	80	000080
oldlace	FD	F5	E6	FDF5E6
olive	80	80	00	808000
olivedrab	6B	8E	23	6B8E23
orange	FF	A5	00	FFA500
orangered	FF	45	00	FF4500
orchid	DA	70	D6	DA70D6
palegoldenrod	EE	E8	AA	EEE8AA
palegreen	98	FB	98	98FB98

Color	Red	Green	Blue	RGB Triplet
paleturquoise	AF	EE	EE	AFEEEE
palevioletred	DB	70	93	DB7093
papayawhip	FF	EF	D5	FFEFD5
peachpuff	FF	DA	B9	FFDAB9
peru	CD	85	3F	CD853F
pink	FF	C0	CB	FFC0CB
plum	DD	A0	DD	DDA0DD
powderblue	B0	E0	E6	B0E0E6
purple	80	00	80	800080
red	FF	00	00	FF0000
rosybrown	BC	8F	8F	BC8F8F
royalblue	41	69	E1	4169E1
saddlebrown	8B	45	13	8B4513
salmon	FA	80	72	FA8072
sandybrown	F4	A4	60	F4A460
seagreen	2E	8B	57	2E8B57
seashell	FF	F5	EE	FFF5EE
sienna	A0	52	2D	A0522D
silver	C0	C0	C0	C0C0C0
skyblue	87	CE	EB	87CEEB
slateblue	6A	5A	CD	6A5ACD
slategray	70	80	90	708090
snow	FF	FA	FA	FFFAFA
springgreen	00	FF	7F	00FF7F
steelblue	46	82	B4	4682B4
tan	D2	B4	8C	D2B48C
teal	00	80	80	008080
thistle	D8	BF	D8	D8BFD8
tomato	FF	63	47	FF6347
turquoise	40	E0	D0	40E0D0
violet	EE	82	EE	EE82EE
wheat	F5	DE	B3	F5DEB3
white	FF	FF	FF	FFFFFF
whitesmoke	F5	F5	F5	F5F5F5
yellow	FF	FF	00	FFFF00
yellowgreen	9A	CD	32	9ACD32

Techie Talk

algorithm: An algorithm is a set of instructions designed to solve a problem. An algorithm can be expressed in English or some other human language, or translated into a computer language such as JavaScript.

applet: An applet is a Java program that's specifically designed to be integrated into an HTML file (that is, a Web page). On the other hand, Java programs designed to run as stand-alone applications, such as Hot Java, are called — well, they're just called Java programs.

array: An array is an indexed (or numbered) list of elements. You can create arrays of numbers, strings, and objects. You access an array's elements by using their indexes. For example, if you have an array called `desserts` and you want to access the first element, you type `desserts [0]`; the second element, `desserts[1]`; the third element, `desserts[2]`, and so on. The built-in arrays to which you have access in JavaScript are `anchors`, `elements`, `forms`, `frames`, `links`, and `options`.

blur: When you've clicked with your mouse pointer on a form element, that element is said to have focus. When you then click somewhere else on the Web page, that first element is said to have lost focus (or *blurred*). In JavaScript, some form elements have an `onBlur` event handler associated with them, which you can use to trigger some function when the element blurs. See *focus*.

Boolean: The Boolean datatype (sometimes called *logical* type) is a data type that consists of only two possible values: *true*, which is sometimes represented as 1, and *false*, which is sometimes represented as 0.

CGI: *CGI (Component Gateway Interface)* is a protocol that allows Web servers and Web clients to pass information back and forth to each other. CGI programs are typically written in either Perl or C languages and reside on Web servers. A client-side Web page automatically submits a form to a server-side CGI program when a user clicks on a Submit button. The CGI program is specified as part of the Web page's `<FORM>` declaration.

client: A client is a software application that makes a request, usually for data, from another software application. Although technically no law says that they have to be, client software and server software are usually located on different machines. See *Web client.*

content: A Web page's content is the information that the page contains, whatever that may be — an online magazine article, a product advertisement, a JavaScript example, or what have you. On the Web, authors are referred to as "content providers."

cookie: A cookie is a piece of information about a client process (such as a Web browser session) that CGI server programs can store on the client's machine. Only the server that creates the cookie and the client that stores it have access to the information stored in the cookie. Cookies are saved in a file called `cookies.txt`.

daemon: A daemon is a program that runs in the background on a server machine, waiting for requests. The HyperText Transfer Protocol Daemon, or *httpd,* must be running on a Web server for any Web clients to be able to interact with the server.

focus: When you put your cursor on a form element and click on it, the element becomes active and lets you interact with it. That element is now said to have *focus.* In JavaScript, some form elements have an `onFocus` event handler associated with them, which you can use to trigger some function when the element receives focus. See *blur.*

HTML: *HTML* stands for *HyperText Markup Language.* HTML is a standard language that contains a set of conventions (called *tags*) that you can use to specify the appearance you want for each particular part of your Web document. HTML is supported by all Web browsers, including Navigator and Internet Explorer. All Web pages are written in HTML; some Web pages also include HTML extensions, like the `<SCRIPT>`... `</SCRIPT>` tag pair that enables JavaScript script embedding.

index: An index is a number assigned to each element in an array. The first index of an array always starts with 0 and then increases by one, like so: 0, 1, 2, 3, 4, and so on.

inheritance: Inheritance is the ability of an object-oriented programming language to create an object by substantially reusing another object's characteristics — for example, the ability to create an object called Part-Time Employee from an object called Employee. JavaScript doesn't support inheritance, so it's not considered a true object-oriented language (it *is* considered an object-based language, though).

Internet: The Internet, or 'Net, is a worldwide computer network made up of hardware, software, and communications lines. Different protocols, like *http* and *news,* allow users to peek at content on the Internet in different ways.

interpreter: An interpreter is a piece of software that transforms human-readable source code into machine-readable language. Every JavaScript-enabled Web browser contains a JavaScript interpreter.

Java: Java is an object-oriented programming language designed by Sun Microsystems. Java is similar in some ways to C++. Java was specifically designed to be the ultimate Internet application development language, so it includes built-in features like cross-platform capability and security. You can integrate Java applets into Web pages and, with Netscape Navigator 3.0, you can integrate Java applets into JavaScript scripts.

JavaScript: JavaScript is a C-like scripting language developed by Netscape Communications. JavaScript, implemented as an extension to HTML, makes it possible for developers to create Web pages that respond to user events and perform client-side calculations. At the time of this writing, Netscape Navigator and Microsoft Internet Explorer are the only generally available browsers that support JavaScript.

LiveConnect: Implemented in Netscape Navigator Version 3.0, LiveConnect is the technology from Netscape Communications that allows JavaScript statements to interact directly with Java applets and Netscape plug-ins.

LiveWire: LiveWire (and LiveWire Pro) are server-side integrated tool suites from Netscape Communications that allow users to create, maintain, and manage Web sites. Both LiveWire and LiveWire Pro support compiled versions of JavaScript.

method: A method, sometimes called a *member function,* is a function that is defined specifically for a particular object and operates only on that object's data. Different objects can have methods of the same name (for example, `document.close()` and `window.close()`).

MIME type: *MIME* stands *for Multipurpose Internet Mail Extensions.* MIME types are standard types of multimedia files that can be passed around the Web. Some examples are `audio/x-wav`, `image/jpeg`, and `text/html`.

object: In object-oriented programming languages (or object-based languages like JavaScript), an object is a complex data type that represents a real-world person, place, thing, or idea. Objects can be built-in, like the button, check box, document, radio, and window objects, or they can be custom-defined by a programmer/JavaScript author.

polymorphism: Polymorphism, along with inheritance, is one of the defining characteristics of object-oriented languages. Polymorphism is the ability to call a method with the same name on multiple objects (for example, `document.close()` and `window.close()`, in which the `close()` method can be called on both the `document` and the `window` objects). JavaScript supports polymorphism.

property: A property is a descriptive characteristic of an object. For example, a `Cat` object might logically contain `name`, `size`, `color`, `age`, and `hadShots` properties, with corresponding property values of `"Inky"`, `"small"`, `"black"`, `"3 months"`, `"yes"`. All object properties are accessible via JavaScript statements.

public: The `public` keyword is used in some object-oriented languages to indicate that a particular property or method defined in one class can be called from another class. Public properties and methods of Java applets can be invoked directly from JavaScript statements with Netscape Navigator 3.0.

script: A script is a simple, interpreted computer program that falls about midway on the continuum between command line directives and full-blown programming languages. JavaScript is an example of a scripting language.

server: A server is a software application that answers requests (usually for data) from other software applications, called clients. Clients and servers are typically (but not always) on different machines. See *client* and *Web server.*

source file: A human-readable computer language file that must be either compiled or interpreted in order to run on a computer. JavaScript scripts are embedded into HTML source files and are then interpreted by the HTML interpreter that's integrated into every JavaScript-enabled Web browser. See *interpreter.*

state: The content of an object at any point in time is referred to as the object's state.

string: A string is a collection of characters treated as an entity, usually surrounded by either single or double quotes. The `String` object is built-in to JavaScript and contains such methods as `bold()` and `blink()`.

substring: A substring is some portion of a string.

syntax: Syntax refers to the rules of punctuation and word order of a language. JavaScript, because it's considered a language (a *scripting* language), has its own syntax that must be followed precisely in order to create working JavaScript scripts.

tag: In HTML, a tag is a keyword (like `<TITLE>`, `</TITLE>`, `<BODY>`, and `</BODY>`) that tells the HTML interpreter how to interpret and handle a piece of text. HTML is sometimes referred to as a *tag language.*

template: A template is a skeleton file that contains basic information, as well as placeholders for customized information. Many programmers use templates as the basis of their source files (including HTML source files) so that they don't have to keep typing in the boring, essential statements common to every source file.

`this`: When encountered within a form element, `this` refers to the specific instance of that form element. It's a kind of shorthand that you can use to avoid typing a very long form element name over and over.

transaction: A transaction is an instance of communication between a calling program and a called program. A transaction begins when communication initiates and ends when the communication ceases. A transaction is sort of like a conversation between two computer programs.

URL: A Uniform Resource Locator is a path name for objects on the Web. For example, `http://www.idgbooks.com` is a URL.

Web: An abbreviation for the World Wide Web, the Web is a huge conglomeration of text, image, audio, video, and heaven-knows-what-other-kinds-of-media, organized into *Web pages* that are scattered all across the planet on multitudes of *Web servers*. The Web is more than just data, though; it's also the connections between the data as well as the software that lets users access the data.

Web client: A Web client is a computer, typically a personal computer running the Macintosh or Windows operating systems. A Web client has a Web browser installed and running (like Netscape Navigator or Internet Explorer).

Web page: A Web page, sometimes referred to as a Web application, is a file written in HTML (and possibly HTML extensions, like JavaScript) that may display text, sound, graphics, movies, and interactive forms to any user who accesses the Web page.

Web server: A Web server is computer, typically running UNIX. A Web server has something called *httpd* (HyperText Transfer Protocol Daemon) installed and running on the server. Web servers store Web pages and CGI programs, which are accessed and used by Web clients.

Web site: A Web site is a collection of linked Web pages, produced by the same individual or company.

wizard: A wizard is a software utility that greatly speeds the completion of a task. A wizard questions a user and then automatically does something based on the user's answers. An example of a wizard is the Netscape Powerstart Setup page, which lets you choose content and layout for your very own customized home page and then constructs the page for you.

WYSIWYG: What You See Is What You Get (pronounced "wizzie-wig"). WYSIWYG HTML editors, such as Microsoft Internet Assistant, are Web page editors that let you drag and drop text to create HTML files instead of having to type in the HTML tags yourself.

Index